Johann Heinrich Alsted, John Birchensbach

Templum musicum

Or the Musical Synopsis of the Learned and Famous Johannes Henricus

Alstedius

Johann Heinrich Alsted, John Birchensbach

Templum musicum
Or the Musical Synopsis of the Learned and Famous Johannes Henricus Alstedius

ISBN/EAN: 9783744657327

Printed in Europe, USA, Canada, Australia, Japan

Cover: Foto ©Thomas Meinert / pixelio.de

More available books at **www.hansebooks.com**

To Musick's sacred Temple, Mercurie,
And Orpheus dedicate their Harmonie
From thence proceeding. Whose faire Handmaids are
Mysterous Numbers: which, if you compare,
The Rat'on of proport'ons you will find.
These please the Eare, and Satisfie the mind.
For nothing, more, the Soule and sense contents,
Then Sounds express'd by voice, and Instruments.

TEMPLUM MUSICUM:
OR THE
MUSICAL SYNOPSIS,
OF
The Learned and Famous
Johannes - Henricus - Alstedius,
BEING
A *Compendium* of the *Rudiments*
both of the *Mathematical* and
Practical Part of
MUSICK:
Of which Subject not any Book is extant in our English Tongue.

Faithfully tranflated out of Latin
By *John Birchensha.* Philomath.

Imprimatur, *Feb.* 5. 1663.

Roger L'Eftrange.

London, Printed by *Will.* *Godbid* for *Peter Dring* at the *Sun* in the *Poultrey* next Dore to the *Rofe-Tavern.* 1664.

To the Right Honourable

EDVVARD *Lord* MONTAGU

Earl of *Sandwich,* &c.

Knight of the *moſt Noble Order* of
the *Garter*, and One of His
Majeſties moſt Honourable
Privy-Council.

SIR,

WHen I conſidered the
Excellency of the
Subject of this *Book,*
and deſerved Fame
of the learned *Author,* I thought
it not neceſſary to crave a Pro-
tection

tection for this *Treatiſe* by a *Dedication* of it unto any : being in it ſelf far above the reach of detracting *Calumniators.* Yet I have made bold, humbly, to preſent it to your Honour as a pleaſant and delightful Divertiſement from your many and great Imployments. In all Ages *Muſick* hath been acceptable to the wiſeſt, greateſt, and moſt Learned men , of whom many have been famous for their great Ability and Knowledge in this *Science* and *Art.* It was no diſpraiſe to *David* that he plaid *skilfully* on the *Harp,* and *Sang* well: the Compo-

Compofitions of divers *German* Princes are extant : neither is it the leaft of thofe Virtues which are eminent in your Lordfhip, that you are both a Lover of *Mufick*, and a good *Mufician*. The renowned *Alftedius* in this *Compendium* (not much differing in his Judgement from the Opinion of the Generality of modern mufical *Claffic's*)does prefent the world with a great Light and Difcovery of this Art, with the *Subject*, *Principle* and *Affections* thereof, with the curious *Symmetry* of Proportions : the proportional Dimenfions of *Sounds :*

Sounds : the Variety of *Diaf-tems :* the admirable *Series* of muficalVoices : the ufefulneffe of *Tetrachords :* the feveral *Genus's* of *Mufick :* and harmonical *Moods*, which being expreffed by *Voice* or *Inftrument* or both, do operate incredibly upon the *Affections.* Wherefore I hope that this *Book* will be accepted both by your *Honour*, and all ingenuous Lovers and Profeffors of this *Art*, and the *Errors* thereof favourably pardoned by your Lordfhip and them. The *Reafon* which moved me to undertake this *Tranflation*, was, becaufe

cauſe I deſired a Diſcovery
might be made of ſome Principles of the *Mathematical* part
of *Muſick*, unto thoſe ingenuous Lovers of this *Science*,
who underſtand only our own
Language , to the End that
by this means the tranſcendent
Virtue and Excellency that is
comprehended in the due proportions of muſical *Sounds* may
be known unto them ; which
will give Satisfaction unto their
Reaſon aſwell as to their *Sence.*
I do not think this unworthy
my labour, becauſe that many
skilful Muſicians have not
thought it any Diſparagement

to

to publifh their *Tranflations* of the Works of famous Men, who did write of the *Art* which they themfelves profeffed. As *Meibomius* Tranflated fome Fragments of *Baccheus*, *Alyppius*, *Nichomachus*, and others: the never to be forgotten *Franchinus*, the Commentaries of *Briennius*, *Ariftides*, *Ptolomy*, and others: and our *Englifh Douland*, the *Introduction* of *Ornithoparcus*. In the Author's laft *Edition* of his univerfal *Encyclopædia*, I met with an *Appendix* to his Mufical *Synopfis*, taken out of the writings of *Erycius Puteanus*; but not finding
ing

ing any thing new in it, only an *ABCdary Repetition* of the firſt Elements of *Muſick,* formerly but more judiciouſly and largely handled in this *Compendium:* and alſo ſome few *Queſtions* ſtarted by *Cardanus,* which are, for the moſt part more fully and Satisfactorily reſolved by the Author; I did forbear the Tranſlation thereof; not being willing to weary the *Reader* with the unneceſſary recital of thoſe things, nor your Lordſhip with too tedious an Epiſtle, which I here conclude, humbly craving pardon for my boldneſſe, and your Honours favourable

favourable Acceptation of this
Mite from your Lordships

Most humble

and devoted

Servant,

JOHN BIRCHENSHA.

To all ingenious L o v e r s of
MUSICK.

G E N T L E M E N ,

*T was for your Profit and Bene-
fit that I undertook this
Translation : and that you
might thereby understand the
Rudiments and Principles both
of the Mathematical and
Practical Parts of this Science. We know that there is
some light into the Mathe-
matical Part of all other Arts ; but little discovery
of that Part of the Theory of Musick hath been made
in our Language ; therefore I did suppose that this
work would be gratefully accepted by you , the Author
having more fully discovered the Precepts , Rules ,
and Axioms of this Science , then any other whose
Works I have seen.*

*Since the Rumour of this Translation hath been
spred abroad , I have by diverse been demanded,* What
Benefit and Advantage the Knowledge of the Mathematical Part of Musick does contribute to the
completing of a Musician ? *To which I answer,That
it is as necessary for a perfect and complete Musician to*
under-

understand the Proportion of Sounds, as for a curious Painter, exactly to know the Symmetry of every part of a Body: that so he may rightly understand the ground and foundation of the Art he does profess, which is, the nature of Sounds, and their due Proportion, in respect of their Ration, Habitude, Quality, Difference, Excess, Dimension, and Magnitude. For this I dare boldly affirm, and if Occasion be offered, undertake to prove it: That such Rules may be yet further, and are already, in part, contrived (drawn from the Mathematical Principles of Musick, by which, musical Consonants and Dissonants (artificially applied and disposed, according to the nature of their Proportions, and by the forementioned Canons) may afford, in 2, 3, 4, 5, 6, 7, or more parts, as good Musick, that is, as agreeable, artificial, and formal, as can be composed by the help of any Instrument. Yet until such Rules be known, it is commendable in any to use such helps as may Advantage their Compositions. But for any Musician to undervalue or speak slightly of the Mathematical part of Musick, is to reproach the Common Parent from whom the Art he professeth received a Being. I know that all Ingenuous persons who are Artists, will acknowledge that it is a more noble way to work by Rules and Precepts in any Art, then mechanically; And so to work in this Art. i. e. to compose regularly, will be found more advantagious then any other way in these Respects. For by such a way of Operation the Composer shall work more certainly, firmly, readily, and with more facility then by any other way.

If Musick be an Art, then it may be contracted

and

and collected into certain Rules which may discover all those Mysteries that are contained in that Science, by which a man may become an excellent Musician, and expert, both in the Theorical and Practical Parts thereof. To the Completeing of such forcible Rules I have contributed my Mite, whose Certainty and Reality has been Experienced by divers, and may likewise be further known unto others, if they please or desire to understand them.

I know that all Virtuoso's will encourage those things which conduce to the Improvement of any ingenious Art: but what shall be spoken against such things by persons rude, envious, or that do pass their Judgement rashly upon things which they know not, having neither seen, heard, nor understood them, is not to be valued. And I do assure my self that there is not any person in this Nation, that is a true Lover of this Science; or a Professour thereof, who does truely honour and understand this Art, but could cordially wish such an Improvement thereof, that those things which in Musick are concealed and mysterious, might be fully discovered: those which are imperfect, completed: those which are doubtful and disputable, cleared by evident Demonstration: those which are not to be done without great trouble, facilitated: those many Observations which burthen the Memory, made few and plain: and those whose Operation and Experience do's require the study and Expence of many years, might be performed without any difficulty in a few Weeks, or Months at the farthest. And that this way is found out and effected in a great measure, I say, many persons of Worth and Quality are able experimentally to testifie. Musick

To the Reader.

Musick hath already flowed to a great Leighth in this Nation, for I am perswaded that there is as much Excellency in the Musick which hath been, and is now composed in England, as in any part of the World, for Ayre, variety and Substance. But I heartily wish, that after this great Spring and Flood, there be not (in our succeeding Generations) as low an Ebb. For if the serious and substantial part of Harmony be neglected, and the mercurial only used: It will prove volatile, evaporate, and come to nothing. But, Gentlemen, I would not willingly weary your patience, and since the Temple *is so small, I will not make the Gate too bigg; But subscribe my self as it is known I am) a true Lover of Musick, and*

Your Servant

J. B.

I Have endeavoured faithfully to translate the Original, in which I find some mistakes, which I dare not impute to the Author, of which I would have thee take notice. And also one Erratum in this Impression.

1. Fol. 20. *the greater Semitone exceedeth the lesser by the lesser Diesis: whereas it exceedeth it but by a Comma, as appeareth* fol. 18. *where the Author saith thus,* The Comma is the difference between the Semitone major and minus.

2. Fol. 31. *almost ten parallel Lines; the Word* almost *should be left out, for the greater System is ten parallel Lines.*

3. Fol. 44. *for* d moll. *read* b moll.

TEMPLUM MUSICUM,

CHAP. I.

Of the Subject of MUSICK.

PRECEPTS.

MUSICK is the Science of Singing well, otherwife called Harmonical: and Mufathena.

The parts thereof are two : the general and the fpecial.

The general part doth treat of the Subject of Mufick ; and both of the Principles and Affections of the Subject.

The Subject of Mufick is an harmonical Song. And this is the Subject of Tractation. The Subject of Informa-

tion,

tion, is the Faculty of Singing : and the Subject of Operation, is the matter to which harmonical Musick may be applied.

Rules.

1. Musick *is a Mathematical Science, subalternate to Arithmetick.*

For as *Arithme*[...]oth treat of *Number*, so *Musick* of the number of *Sounds :* Or as others of numerous *Sound.* For as the *Optick Science* is called a certain special *Geometrie* , so *Musick* may be called a certain special *Arithmetick :* But whereas some contend that *Musick* is both a *Science*, *Prudence*, and *Art*, because it doth instruct both skilfully, or scientifically, and prudently, and artificially to compose an harmonical Song, it is not so accurate. For it is not here Queried, whether *Science*, *Prudence*, and *Art* may concur in Practise : but whether *Musick* being considered as a *Discipline* either habitual or systematical, be a *Science*, *Prudence*, or *Art*. But that it is a *Science* it doth thus appear, because it hath *Subject*, *Principles*, and *Affections* ; which three things are required unto the complete *Ration* of a *Science.*

2. *An*

2. *An Harmonical Song , is a con-
cinnous multitude of Sounds , rightly
compofed according to the Text.*

The Subject of *Explication* in *Mufick* is a *Song*,
whofe chief *Force* lieth in this , that it is accommodated to the *Text* and *Affections.*

But if the fame *Sound* may be accommodated to
divers and contrary things and Affections , then the
Mufick is inept and irrational ; becaufe it is contrary
to the Scope and Principle of that moft laudable
Difcipline, which will , That *Melodie* be applied
both to *Things* and *Affections.*

If therefore *v. g.* in any Pfalm of *David*, three
Parts do occur , *viz. Lamentation , Confolation ,*
and giving of *Thanks :* there, three *Tones* ought to
be.

3. *The Subject of Operation in Mufick
are Things facred and liberal. By
which it appeareth that the ufefulneffe of it is very great.*

Things facred, as the *Pfalms* and *Songs* in the
Bible, and of other things wholly Divine.

Things liberal, as *pathetical* matters in things
Philofophical , and which doth altogether concern
the common Life of Man. For *Mufick* doth pene-

trate

trate the Interiors of the mind, it moveth Affections, promoveth Contemplation, expelleth Sorrow, diſſolveth bad Humours, exhilerateth the animal Spirits: and ſo is beneficial to the Life of Men in general, to the Pious for Devotion, to the Contemplative Life for Science, to the Solitary for Recreation, to the domeſtick and publick Life for Moderation of mind, to the Healthful for the temperament of their Body, and to the cheerful for Delight; As excellently ſaith that famous Muſician *Lippius* in his Muſical *Synopſis.* Hence it is that the Divel hateth Muſick liberal, and on the contrary is delighted with filthy Muſick and illiberal, which he uſeth as his Vehicle, by which he ſlideth himſelf into the minds of men, who take Pleaſure in ſuch Diabolical Muſick. On the contrary, the holy Angels are delighted with Muſick liberal, not becauſe corporal Harmony doth affect them, but becauſe all Harmony, eſpecially that which is conjoyned with the Affection of a pious *Will*, is grateful to thoſe chaſt Spirits. Hence it is, that the *Heroes*, holy Men, and Lovers of Virtue of all times, have magnified Muſick: as appeareth by theſe Scriptures; *Exod.* 15. *Judg.* 5. 1. 1 *Sam.* 16. 23. 2 *Sam.* 6. 5. 2 *Kings* 3. 15. 1 *Chron.* 23. 5. *Judith* 16. 1, 2, &c. *Syrach* 22. 5, 6, & 39. 20. & 44. 5. *Matth.* 26. 30. *Luke* 1. 46. & 2. 13. *Eph.* 5. 18, 19. *Col.* 3. 16. *Apoc.* 5. 9. & 14. 2, 3.

CHAP. II.

✠✠✠✠✠✠✠✠✠✠✠✠✠✠✠✠✠✠✠✠✠✠

Chap. II.

Of the Principles of Cognition in Muſick.

Precepts.

THE Principles of an Harmonical Song are thoſe things upon which it doth depend : And thoſe are either the Principles of the Cognition or Conſtitution thereof.

Thoſe are complex : theſe incomplex.

The Principles of Cognition are thoſe by which an harmonical Song is known. And they are either internal or external. Thoſe are taken from the Science it ſelf, theſe from Philoſophy, partly theorctical, and partly practical.

Rules.

1. *The internal or domeſtical Princi-*
ples of Cognition are here and there
ſpread through the whole Body of
Muſick. Wherefore it were not worth while
to treat of them in this place.

2. *The theoretical Principles which*
Muſick doth uſe, or is built upon,
are either remote or proximate.

The remote are ſuch as are taken from the *Me-*
taphyſicks and *Phyſicks.* And indeed from the *Me-*
taphyſicks, there are taken Principles of Unity,
Goodneſſe, Pulchritude, Perfection, Order, Oppoſition, Quantity, Quality, and the like. And
from the *Phyſicks*, thoſe that treat of the Quantity,
Quality, Motion, Place, and Time of a natural
Body: Alſo of Air, and Sound, and of its propa-
gation, multiplication, differences, and percep-
tion: And laſtly of Affections, as Love, Joy, Sorrow, and the like. The proximate principles are
Axioms, Aſſumptions, Queſtions, Theorems, Pro-
blems, and Confectaries mathematical; and thoſe
partly arithmetical, partly geometrical: but chiefly
arithmatical; eſpecially thoſe which concern the Pro-
prieties

prieties of Simple Numbers , and also their proportion ; *viz. dupla , tripla, sesquialtera,* and the
like , of which in my Arithmeticks : But here let
these *Axioms* be obferved. 1. That Proportion of
Equality is radically between one and one : And this
is the Radix of all Proportion. 2. *Dupla* Proportion is radically between two and one , *tripla* between three and one , *quadrupla* between four and
one , and fo forward. Obferve , that radical proportions are in Nine Simple Numbers, from 1. to 9.
becaufe thefe are the Radixes of all Numbers. 3.
Sesquialtera Proportion is between three and two ,
Sesquitertia between four and three, *Superbipartiens
tertias,* is radically between five and three, and *Supertripartiens quintas* is between eight and five. And
thefe are fimple proportions, in which fuch an order of perfection is obferved , that after a proportion of Equality , a proportion of inequality followeth : Firft *Dupla,* afterward *Sesquialtera,* then *Sesquitertia,* afterward *Sesquiquarta,* and *Sesquiquinta,*
then *Superbipartiens tertias* , and *Supertripartiens
quintas.* To thefe fucceed compounded Proportions,
as *Dupla-Sesquialtera* between 5, and 2. *Tripla-Ses-
quitertia* between 10, and 3. *Dupla-Superbipartiens
tertias* , as between 8, and 3. and fo forward. 4.
Proportions are numbred by Divifion logiftical , as
the proportion which is between 3, 2. appeareth by
Divifion. For if 3. be divided by 2. it will pro-
duce 1. $\frac{1}{2}$. 5. Proportions are added by vulgar mul-
tiplication , as $\frac{3}{2}$: $\frac{7}{2}$: make $\frac{6}{2}$: $\frac{7}{2}$: 6. Proportions are
fubftracted by Multiplication crucial ; as $\frac{^{3}X^{1}}{_{4} ^{}}$

7. Proportions are multiplied or coupled when they are written without Intermiffion, and the antecedent number of the latter proportion is multiplied into the Confequent of the former, or contrarily. Alfo when the Confequent of the former is multiplied into the Confequent of the latter. Or laftly, when the Antecedent of the former is multiplied into the antecedent of the pofterior. As 2. 1, 3, 2. Here, once three, give three: and once two, give two, and twice three, give fix. 8. Proportions are radicated in greater numbers, and in numbers compounded one with another by Mediation logiftical; as 16-8. Firft they are reduced to 8-4. then to 4-2. laftly to 2-1. And thus radical Proportions by courfe are eafily reduced to their greater Terms by logiftical *Duplation*; as 1-2. to 2-4. thence to 4-8. then to 8-16. and fo forward. 9. Every *Dupla* Proportion doth confift of a *Sefquialtera* and *Sefquitertia*. 10. If a *Sefquialtera* be taken away from a *Dupla*, a *Sefquitertia* will only remain, and fo confequently.

3. *Practical Principles which Mufick ufeth, are chiefly taken from the Ethicks, Oeconomicks, Politicks, and Poeticks.*

From the *Ethicks* are taken Principles of Virtue, and moral Beatitude; from the *Oeconomicks* of Actions

ons domeſtick ; from *Politicks* Principles of virtue,
and civil Beatitude; and from *Poetrie* Principles concerning Rhyme and Verſe : which have ſuch Affinity
with Muſick , that by ſome Muſick is divided into
Harmonical , Rhythmical , and Metrical.

⊕⊕⊕⊕⊕⊕⊕⊕⊕⊕⊕⊕⊕⊕⊕⊕⊕⊕⊕⊕⊕⊕⊕⊕⊕⊕⊕⊕⊕

C H A P. III.

Of the Efficient and End of an Harmonical Song.

PRECEPTS.

THE Principles of Conſtitution are
thoſe by which an harmonical Song
is conſtituted.

And they are either external oꝛ internal.

The external are the Efficient and End.
The Efficient Cauſe of a Song is either
the firſt oꝛ ſecond.

The firſt Cauſe is GOD the Authoꝛ of
all Symphony.

The ſecond is partly Nature, the Mother

ther of all Sounds : partly Art perfecting
the Rudiment of Nature.

The ultimate End is GOD that Archetype of Harmony.

The ſubordinate End is Motion , and
the impulſe of Man to the hatred of Uice,
and ſtudy of Uirtue.

Rules.

1. *God is the Author and Maintainer of all Harmony,*

Seeing Harmony is Order, and tendeth to Unity ;
for God is the Author and Maintainer of all Order ,
and the greateſt Unity. Furthermore , God is the
chief and unſpeakable Joy, therefore they who rightly
rejoyce come nigher unto God. Hence the *Rabbins*
ſay, *the Holy Ghoſt doth ſing by reaſon of Joy.* And
Philoſophers ſay , *That the Soul of a Wiſe man doth
alwayes rejoyce* ; For joy as it is pure Harmony cannot but be excited and maintained by Muſical Harmony.

2. *The*

2. *The Exemplary Cause of Harmonical Music; is that Music which is called mundane.*

This is difcerned in the Order, Difpofition, and admirable proportion which doth occur in the Celeftial, and fubceleftial Region; partly among the Stars, partly among the Elements, partly among all things compounded of the Elements; and laftly, among all thofe things which are compared one with another: of which Mufick and Harmony we have fpoken in our *Phyficks*. This Harmony being fuch and fo great, when ancient men did diligently confider it, they fuppofed that there was the like Proportion not only in Numbers and Lines, but alfo in the Voice; efpecially when they did difcern that Proportion in the various Sound of various Bodies.

3. *Music receiveth his greateft Perfection from the End.*

That Perfection doth not only depend upon matter and Form, but alfo upon the End we have formerly fhewn in our *Metaphyficks* and *Logicks*. In *Mufick* certainly this is moft manifeft: for unlefie it be referred to the Glory of God, and the pious Recreation of Man it cannot but equivocally be called Mufick. Hence it is apparent that thofe fimple men who abufe Vocal and Inftrumental Mufick to

nourifh

nouriſh the pleaſures of this World, whilſt they ſing Songs highly obſcene, are nothing leſſe then *Muſi-cians.* For although the Form of a Song occur there, yet the End which perfecteth the Inſtrument, is not there diſcerned: Therefore in ſuch Muſick there is the firſt perfection but not the ultimate ; which nece-ſſarily is required in an Inſtrument, becauſe the Virtue thereof is placed in the uſe.

⊕⊕⊕⊕⊕⊕⊕⊕⊕⊕⊕⊕⊕⊕⊕⊕⊕⊕⊕⊕⊕⊕⊕⊕

Chap. IV.

Of the quantity of a Muſical Song.

Precepts.

THE internal **Principles** of an **har-monical Song** are **Matter** and **Form.**

Matter comprehendeth the integral parts of which an **Harmonical Song** is made.

Of the parts thereof, the one is **Sim-ple,** and the other is compounded.

The

The ſimple part is called Sound : alſo a Muſical Monad. in Greek Tonos.

A Muſical Sound is conſidered in reſpect of his Quantity and Signs.

The Doctrine of that is called theoretical Muſick , and of this Signatory.

Quantity is threefold, Longitude, Latitude, and Craſſitude.

The Longitude of a Muſical Sound , is that which is diſcerned in the motion and Duration thereof : and meaſured by a Muſical Touch or Tact.

The Latitude of a Muſical Sound is that which is diſcerned in the tenuous and aſperous ſpirit.

The Craſſitude of a Muſical Sound is that which is diſcerned in the Profundity and Altitude thereof.

By reaſon of this Craſſitude a Muſical Sound is equal or unequal.

The equal Sound is the Simple Uniſon.

The unequal Sound doth bring forth a Diſtance or an Interval of a ſonorous Craſſitude : which is called a Muſical Interval.

B

A Muſical Interval is ſeen in Propor=
tion and Intention.

By reaſon of Proportion, an Interval
is ſimple or compounded: that is called
radical, this radicated.

A Simple Interval is either Juſt, or
not Juſt.

A Juſt Interval is that which is nei=
ther defective nor redundant: as an Octave
Fifth, &c.

An Interval not Juſt is that which is
defective or redundant: as a Semioctave,
&c.

A compounded Interval is that which
doth conſiſt of ſimple Intervals: as a
double Octave, a triple Octave, a qua-
druple Octave, and ſo ad infinitum.

By reaſon of Intention it is a Scale,
called Muſical; and it is the various diſ=
poſition of acute and grave Sounds.

Rules.

1. *Every Sound is Quantus.*

For in every Body that hath Quantity, there is an
audible Quality. That Quantity is numbred by Divifion, and not barely confidered, as it is a magnitude. So that the moft accurate *Lippius* might rightly
fay, every Sound is continual or difcrete, or explain-
able by number. But a Sound is *Quantus*, by complete Quantity. *i. e.* So that it have a trine Dimen-
fion, and therefore Longitude, Latitude, and
Craffitude.

2. *Every Sound is long numerably.*

For feeing every Sound doth continue fo long, or
not fo long, this temporal duration thereof may be
numbred. And it is numbred by a Mufical *Touch*,
which, according to the motion of the Heart, in
this Science ought to be obferved. This Touch doth
confift of *Depreffion* and *Elevation*, according to a
certain Proportion, but efpecially a *Dupla:* And it
is either more fimple, more natural, and more common, which is finifhed in two equal parts, and may
be called *Spondaic*, as Mfs Īs: or leffe fimple, and
more unufual, which doth confift of unequal parts,
the one greater, and the other lefter, and may be
called *Trochaic*, as Mfs ă.

3. *Every*

3. *Every Sound is numerably broad.*

For every Sound beſides the length thereof, is alſo tenuous or gentle, flat, ſubmiſs, ſmall; or ſharp, harſh, clear, full, as conſiſting of a tenuous and aſperous Spirit.

4. *Every Sound is numerably thick.*

Beſides the length and breadth, every Sound is alſo thick; and ſo it is either deep or high. That, is called grave, and this, acute. And we meaſure this magnitude of a Sound by Proportions of numbers, eſpecially radical, as they are applied to the *Monochord.*

5. *The Simple Uniſon is the Principal and Radix of all Muſical Intervals.*

As in numbers there is one proportion of Equality, and another of Inequality: So alſo in Sounds, one is equal, and another is unequal. And again as in numbers, the Proportion of Equality is the *Radix* of all the reſt: So in Sounds, the Simple Uniſon is the principal and *Radix* of all Muſical *Intervals.* For the Simple Uniſon doth conſiſt of a proportion of Equality, which is radically between 1. and 1. as may be ſeen in a *Monochord.* Therefore a Simple Uniſon is not a muſical Interval, but the original thereof.   6. *Unequal*

6. *Unequal Sounds do make a Mufic Intervall.*

Unequal Sounds do make a *Diaftem* or *Diftance*, which is called a Mufical Intervall, in which the grave Sound is profound and greater : and the acute, high and leffer. Of this intervall thefe *Theorems* are noted. 1. *He that knoweth a fimple Intervall, may eafily know a compounded Intervall.* That, as they fay, is radical : this, radicated. 2. *There are feventeen fimple Intervals or Diaftems in this order.* The firft, an *Octave*, to wit, a voice, in Greek a *Diapafon*, which is of a *Dupla* Proportion, between 2. and 1. where one Sound as the greater and graver, doth contain another, as the leffer and acuter, twice in it felf; Therefore is the *Unifon* compofed from Letter to Letter, *v. g.* from *G.* to *g.* &c. The fecond, a *Fifth*, or *Diapente*, which is of a *Sefquialtera* Proportion ; between 3. and 2. The third, a *Fourth*, or *Diateffaron*, which is of a *Sefquitertian* Proportion between 4. and 3. The fourth, a greater *Third* or *Ditone*, which is of *Sefquiquarta* Proportion, between 5. and 4. The fifth, a *Third minor*, or *Hemiditone*, which is of *Sefquiquinta* Proportion, between 6. and 5. The fixth, a *Sexta major* [or greater *Sixth*] or fourth with the greater third, which is of a *Superbipartiens tertias* Proportion, as between 5. and 3. 7. A *Sexta minor* or fourth with the leffer *Third*, which is of a *Supertripartiens quintas* Proportion, between 8. and 5. The eigth, is the *major Second*, or whole Tone, which

C   is

is of a *Sefquioctave* Proportion , between 9. and 8. The ninth , is the *minor* Second , or *minor Tone* , of a *Sefquinona* Proportion , between 10. and 9. The tenth , is the *major Semitone* , of the Proportion of 16. and 15. The eleventh , is the *minor Semitone*, of a *Sefquivicefima quarta* Proportion, between 25. and 24. The twelfth , the *Diefis minor* , of a *fupertripartiens centefimas vigefimas quintas* Proportion between 128. and 125. The thirteenth , a *Comma* which is the difference between the *Semitone majus* , and *minus*, of a *Sefquioctogefima* Proportion , be- tween 81. and 80. The fourteenth , a *Schifma* which is the half of a *Comma* , or half of the Dif- ference between the *Semitone majus* and *minus*. The fifteenth , is the fifth with a *tertia major*, or greater *Seventh*, which is of a *Superfeptipartiens octavas* Pro- portion , as between 15. and 8. The fixteenth, is the leſſer *Seventh*, or *quinta cum tertia minore*, which is a *Superquadripartiens quintas* Proportion, between 9. and 5. The feventeenth, are Intervalls not juſt, which are either deficient or redundant , chiefly by the leſſer *Semitone* , or *Comma* , or both together : as the *Semioctave* deficient and abounding *Fifth :* the minute and fuperfluous fourth which is named a *Tri- tone* , and fuch like. 3. *Intervalls compounded of fimple Diaftems may be infinite.* But it is proper to *Mufick* to bound that Infinity of groſs Sounds (which is fuch only potentially.) Notwithſtanding let us take notice of certain compounded *Intervalls.* Firſt, fuch as are once compounded , as a *Difdiapafon*, double *Octave* , or *Fifteenth* , which is of a *quadru- pla* Proportion , between 4. and 1. Alſo a *Diapa-*

ſa

ſon with a *Diapente* , an *Octave* , with a *Fifth* , or *Twelfth* , of a triple Proportion, between 3. and 1. Alſo a *Diapaſon* with a *Diateſſaron* , an *Octave* with a *Fourth*, or *Eleventh* , of a *dupla ſuperbipartiens tertias* Proportion , between 8. and 3. Alſo others are twice compounded , as a *Trisdiapaſon* , *Triple Octave*, or two and twentieth of an *Octupla* Proportion , between 8. and 1. *&c.* Thirdly , others are thrice compounded , as a *Tetradiapaſon* , *quadrupla Octave* , or nine and twentieth of a *ſedecupla* Proportion , between 16. and 1. Others are four times compounded, and ſo *ad infinitum*. 4. *An Octave is the moſt ſimple , perfect , and prime muſical Intervall.* 5. *An Octave divided begets all other ſimple Diaſtems.* Therefore from the Diviſion of the Octave , the Harmonies of every Genus do flow. For every *Octave* being divided two wayes , begetteth two Moóds of it ſelf. 6. *An Octave is firſt divided into a fifth and fourth, of which it doth conſiſt : and that either by harmonical or arithmetical Diviſion. That is called the harmonical Medium of an Octave , when the fifth is beneath the fourth: and that the arithmetical , when the fourth is beneath the fifth.* Let this be the Example of Harmonical Diviſion.

But I ſuppoſe the Author means thus :

Therfore in the harmonical Divifion of an *Octave*
the *fifth* remaining immoveable, the *fourth* is placed above the *fifth* : in the arithmetical Divifion, the
fifth remaining immoveable, the *fourth* is put beneath
the *fifth*. 7. *If a Fifth be taken from an Eighth, there
remaineth a Fourth*, and fo on the contrary. 8. *A
Fifth is divided into a Ditone, and Semiditone*. 9. *A
Ditone is compounded of the greater and leffer Tone*
10. *The* Tonus major *is difpofed into the* Semitone
majus *and* minus. 11. *The Ditone is more then the*
Semiditone *by the* Semitone minus. 12. *A Fourth
exceedeth a Ditone by the* major Semitone. 13. *A
Fifth is more then a Fourth by the greater Tone.* 14.
The leffer Tone is exceeded by the greater by a Comma. 15. *The greater Semitone exceedeth the leffer
by the leffer Diefis.* 16. *A Sixth is made of a Fourth
and a Third, the greater of the greater, and leffer
of the leffer, or the greater of a fifth and leffer Tone,
and the leffer of the* Semitone major. 17. *The fe-
venth* major, *is made of a Fifth and greater Third,
the* minor, *of the* minor. 18. *The greater Tone
doth contain almoft* ten Comma's, *the leffer almoft*
nine ; *the greater Semitone almoft five, and the leffer
almoft four.* 19. *A fifth doth contain two greater
Tones, one leffer, and the* Semitone majus : *A fourth*
one

one greater and leſſer Tone, and the Semitone
majus. Therefore an *Octave* hath in it ſelf ſix
Tones, three *major,* and three *minor,* with the leſſer *Dieſis :* to wit, five Tones, three greater, and
two leſſer, with two *major Semitones,* and ſo it doth
comprehend more then fifty *Comma's.* 20. *Compounded Intervalls do imitate the nature of their ſimple.*
A *Diſdiapaſon* ariſeth from two *Octaves,* an *Octave*
with a *Fifth* comprehendeth eight Tones, five *major,* three *minor,* and three greater *Semitones.* A
Triſdiapaſon is divided into three *Octaves,* and ſo
of the reſt. Theſe Propoſitions are demonſtrated by
propoſitions arithmetical of proportions added, ſub-
ſtracted, coupled, *&c. v. gr.* An *Octave* is of a
dupla proportion, a *Fifth* of a *Seſquialtera,* a
Fourth of a *Seſquitertia.* Therefore an *Octave* doth
conſiſt of a *Fifth* and a *Fourth.* This whole matter
is demonſtrated in a *Monochord :* How theſe things
may be vulgarly propounded, you may ſee hereaf-
ter in the laſt Chapter and laſt Rule.

7. *The Scale of Muſick is explained in theſe Theorems.*

1. *The Series of Intenſion and Remiſſion :* or of
Aſcenſion from a grave Sound into an Acute, and of
the Deſcenſion from an acute into a grave, is called
the *Scale of Muſick.* 2. *The Scale of Muſick doth*
vary both according to ancient and modern *Muſicians.*
For the *Scale* of the moſt ancient Muſicians, was on-

ly

ly of one *Diapaſon* for radical Simplicity. The Scale
of the *Pythagorians* was of a *Diſdiapaſon*, for the
keeping of Mediocrity. And now it is of a *Tris*,
and *Tetra-Diapaſon*, for the grateful variety of vocal and Inſtrumental Muſick. The *Scale* alſo is either Simple: and that either old as the *enharmonic*,
chromatic, and *diatonic*; or new as the *Syntonic*:
or mixed, which is compounded of ſimple[*Intervalls*]
Of theſe the *enharmonic* and *chromatic*, in reſpect
of their Difficulty and imperfection are not uſed in
Solitary Muſick. 3. *The Syntonian Scale is of all
others the moſt harmonical, to which the Diaton Scale
may aptly be mixed:* as it may be ſeen in a *Clavichord*,
and wind Inſtrument, *i. e.* an *Organ*; where the white
Keyes do proceed in the *Syntonian* Scale; which is
ſomewhat moderated by the *Diaton*. The *Syntonian*
Scale proceedeth by the great Tone, the leſſer Tone,
and the greater *Semitone* which ariſeth from the *minor*
Tone: the *diatonic* or *diaton* proceedeth by two *Tones*
and a *Semitone*. To theſe the *enharmonic Scale* is
added, proceeding by two *Dieſes*, the greater and
leſſer, and an immediate *Ditone* in his *Tetrachords*.
Alſo the *chromatic* proceedeth by two *Semitones*,
the greater and the leſſer, and an immediate *Semiditone*. So the black *Keyes* proceed with the white
in the *chromatic*: from whence they are called *fict*
in the *Syntonian*. Hence alſo ariſeth the *Scale* irregular or flat, which differeth not from the regular
or dural, but by accidental *Tranſpoſition*, or by the
fourth above, or by the fifth beneath. And this is
the *Diſpoſition* of the old *diatonic Scale*.

1. *The greater Tone.* 9. 8.
2. *The greater Tone.* 9. 8.
3. *The leſſer Semitone from the greater Tone* 256.243
4. *The greater Tone.* 9. 8.
5. *The greater Tone.* 9. 8.
6. *The greater Tone.* 9. 8.
7. *The leſſer Semitone.* 256. 243.
8. *The greater Tone.* 9. 8. and ſo on through the *Octaves* below and above.

But the Diſpoſition of the new and perfeƈt Syntonian Scale is as followeth ;

1. *The greater Tone.* 9. 8.
2. *The leſſer Tone.* 10. 9.
3. *The greater Semitone.* 16. 15.
4. *The greater Tone.* 9. 8.
5. *The leſſer Tone.* 10. 9.
6. *The greater Tone.* 9. 8.
7. *The greater Semitone.* 16. 15.
8. *The greater Tone.* 9. 8. And ſo on through the *Octaves* above and below.   Compare theſe things with the antecedent Rule, and following Chapters.

✠✠✠✠✠✠✠✠✠✠✠✠✠✠✠✠✠✠✠✠✠✠✠

Chap. V.

Of the Signs of a Muſical Sound.

Precepts.

The Signs of a Muſical Sound do follow.

And thoſe are of a Sound either broad, long, or thick.

The ſignes of a long Sound do note the duration thereof : and they are either principal or leſſe principal.

The principal Signes are a Note and a Pauſe.

A Note is a ſigne of a preſent and poſitive ſound : and containeth Touch, and that either whole or not whole.

It containeth the whole Touch either eight times as a Large, or four times as a Long, or twice as a Breve, or once as a Semibreve.

The reſt do contain not the whole, but part

part of a Touch, and that either the half part as a Minim, or the fourth part as a Crotchet, or the eigth part as a Quaver, or the ſixteenth part as a Semiquaver.

A Pauſe is the Index of a privitive or abſent Sound, that is of ſilence: and it anſwereth either to a Large, or Long, or Breve, &c.

Signes leſſe principal are a ſemicircle with a Center, Cuſtos, or the like.

Signes of a broad ſound, are a prick of Augmentation, breathing, and Syncope: of which, Syncope, is a certain looſing of the Touch; Notes, or Pauſes; breathing anſwereth a Semi-Minim.

The Signes of a Craſſe Sound are parallel Lines, whereof the place and name do occur.

The place is a Muſical Syſtem, and that greater or leſſer.

The greater Syſtem for the moſt part doth conſiſt of ten Lines: and ſerveth for the Compoſing of a Song, called other=wiſe a conjoyned Syſtem.

The leſſer Syſtem doth conſiſt of five Lines, and ſerveth chiefly to a Song pricked out. This is otherwiſe called a ſimple Syſtem.

The

The Name is aſwell a Letter as a Voice, or as others will, a Muſical Syllable.

A Letter is as a Key by which the Song is opened, therefore called Clavis. Such letters are ſeven. A. B. C. D. E. F. G.

The muſical Voices or Syllables are ſix, ut, re, mi, fa, ſol, la.

Theſe are found in a Muſical Scale either continued or diſcontinued.

There, there is no need of Mutation: but here otherwiſe.

R U L E S.

1. *The moſt certain and ready Signs of Sounds are Cyphers of Numbers.*

Becauſe a *Sound* can neither by any Man be written in Paper, nor kept in his Mind, neither only nor alwayes; therefore it ſtandeth in need of certain *Signs*, by which the Quantity and Quality thereof may be repreſented. For becauſe in the Numbers and Proportions of theſe, all the Dimenſions of Sound have their aſſigned Eſſence; the moſt ſure and ready Signs are Cyphers of Numbers placed according

ding to their *Longitude*, *Latitude* , and *Profundity*.
For according to Longitude. 1. 2. 3. 4. 8. $\frac{1}{2}$ $\frac{1}{3}$ $\frac{1}{4}$
may note the ſtay of one Touch , two, three , or
four, *&c.* According to Latitude in like manner ;
and according to Craſſitude the greater Numbers may
ſignifie the grave Sound ; and the leſſer Numbers,
the acute Sound. But it behoveth here to retain vulgar Signs , becauſe they are moſt uſed.

2. *The Doctrine of Notes is contained in theſe Rules.*

1. Notes are either ſimple or compounded. And
thoſe are either whole or broken. Theſe are called
bound. Simple Notes are placed without any joyning of either : Compounded,contrarily.Whole Notes
are meaſured by whole Times ; broken Notes , by
parts of Time. Whole Sounds conſiſt either of one
Time , as a *Semibreve :* or of more , and thoſe either of two , as a *Breve :* four, as a *Long :* or eight,
as a *Large.* The broken Notes do contain either
the ſecond part of a Time , as a *Minem :* or the
fourth , as a *Crotchet :* or the eighth, as a *Quaver :*
or the Sixteenth , as a *Semiquaver.* According to
the following Scheme.

Names.

Names.	Figure.	Value.
Large.		8.
Long.	} *Exceſſus.*	4.
Breve.		2.
Semibreve.	◊ *Medium.*	1.
Minim.		$\frac{1}{2}$
Crotchet.		$\frac{1}{4}$
Quaver.	} *Defectus.*	$\frac{1}{8}$
Semiquaver.		$\frac{1}{16}$

Although more Notes of Longitude may be given, aſwell greater or leſſer, potentially infinite : yet theſe notwithſtanding do ſuffice , which wére invented by Muſicians of former Ages. 2. *Notes are varied according to the Augmentation or Diminution of their value , or according to both together.* Either all or ſome are augmented by the half part;and truely,all are augmented either by the Oppoſition of a Semicircle. C. ₵. and a Prick , of which this is the Rule : A Prick put after Notes doth add the half part of the time above their proper value , as

1 2.   6.   3. $\frac{3}{2}$ $\frac{3}{4}$

Thus

Thus a Prick after a ♮. is a *Monotone*, or ◖. after a
Semibreve is a *Minim* , or ⦙. Some Notes are only augmented by prefixing a Circle **O.** as a *Large* ,
Long , *Breve.* Notes are diminiſhed by a *Trochaic*
Touch in a certain proportion , either *Tripla* or
Seſquialtera. Where the Signs are either Number
or Colour : as ⅓ is *tripla* , ⅔ is *ſeſquialtera.* Notes
are partly augmented and partly diminiſhed , chiefly
by the ligation and obliquation of a *Breve* , which is
done for the extending of one Syllable. And a
Long alſo with a *Breve* is counted for a *Semibreve* ;
and alſo in like manner a *Breve* with a *Breve.* But
this kind of ligation and obliquation is now wholly
omitted , as not neceſſary in the leaſt.

3. *Pauſes meaſuring Silence do anſwer*
   to thoſe muſical Notes whereof they
   are Privations.

For a Pauſe (which is noted by a little Line) doth
anſwer either to a *Large* , or *Long* , or *Breve* , or
other Note : as in the Type.

A

A double Breathing doth anſwer to a *Quaver :* a
Triple to a *Semiquaver.* Hitherto do pertain the
Neuma, Cuſtos, and the like. As

Neuma. Cuſtos.

4. *Signs of a broad Sound are by Ar-tiſts expreſſed leſs carefully.*

The Sign of a broad Sound ought to ſhew the Latitude of it according to the aſperous, harſh, clear,
full, ſoft, flat, and ſmall Spirit thereof, as the
nature of the Text requireth. But Muſicians do leſs
weigh the Latitude of a Sound, and do leave it to
the Text, and to the things themſelves that are to be
ſung, and are content with few Signs, chiefly uſing
breathing and Syncopation. Breathing doth anſwer
to the *Crotchet :* Syncope or Syncopation is a certain
Luxation, that is, a fraction, and Contraction of
Touch, Notes, and Pauſes. *e. gr.*

5. *The Sign of a Craſs Sound is a croſ-ſed Line, as they call it.*

The Sign ſignifying *Craſſitude* of *gravity* and *a-
cutenſſe*

cuteneſſe meaſurable by proportionable *Numbers*, is a perpendicular Line, which a right line doth cut; thus, +. Theſe Lines are called Seats of croſs Sounds or Muſical Intervalls. Alſo a Muſical Syſtem which is twofold, the greater and the leſſer. In both there are perpendicular and parallel Lines; indeed in the greater there are almoſt ten parallel Lines, in the leſſer alwayes five. The greater ſerveth for the compoſing of a Song; where the perpendicular Lines are cut by the diſtance of one or two Touches: But the leſſer doth ſerve for Melody, which is to be extracted and noted.

Let this be the Type of the greater Syſtem.

Let this be the Type of the leſſer Syſtem.

Both theſe Syſtems are put in a Chart, or Melo-poetick *Abacus*, or Compoſitary as they call it. The firſt is convenient to a young Beginner: the latter,

for

for a longer Practitioner : but others would rather
draw more fimple Syftems in an *Abacus* ; Thus,

6. Of Letters and Voices Muſical, as they call them, theſe are the Theorems.

1. The radical Letters are ſeven, in this order,
a. b. c. d. e. f. g. which do moderate Sounds in the
Diatonic Scale of a *Diapaſon.* Theſe are uſually
called Keyes, becauſe that by them a Song is, as it
were, opened. They were invented by *Guido Aretine* ; at this time they are inſufficient.　2. Letters
or Keyes are either *capital, minute,* or *geminate.*
Capital are they which are written with Capital, that
is with great Letters. Thus r. *A. B. C. D. E. F. G.*
of which r. *A. B. C.* are calſed grave, becauſe they
emit a grave Sound in reſpect of the reſt : the reſt,
as *D. E. F. G.* are called finals, becauſe every Song
regularly doth end in theſe Keyes.　We have only

r̃ from the School of the *Greeks.* The minute Keys̄ are in number ſeven, ſo called becauſe they are written with little Letters.   Of theſe *a. b. c. d.* are called affinal, becauſe in theſe Keyes the tranſpoſed Song doth end : otherwiſe called acute, becauſe they do emit a more acute Sound. The other are called *Superacute,* becauſe they are put above the acute, as *e. f. g.* The geminate Keyes are commonly five in number. *aa. bb. cc. dd. ee.* So called becauſe they are written with double Letters.   Otherwiſe called excelling ; becauſe in their Sound they tranſcend all others.   But becauſe the number of Keys is not ſufficient ; therefore latter Muſicians under the great Latin Letters have put ſeven German Letters : and the double Letters they do fully recite, and more-over they add unto them triplicated Letters.   Thus

1.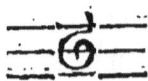

2. *A B C D E F G.*

3. *a b c d e f g.*

4. *aa bb cc dd ee ff gg.*

5. *aaa bbb ccc ddd eee fff ggg.*

3. Keyes are ſigned, or underſtood, or not ſigned: The ſigned Keyes are three which are diſtant one from another by a Fifth, and they are *g. c. f.* thus

D

Theſe

Theſe in the conjoyned Syſtem are thus put , and are diſtant from one another by a *Diapente.*

In a ſimple Syſtem they are variouſly placed by reaſon of the Profundity and Altitude of a Song; As ,

But Keyes not ſigned are known by the ſigned.

4. *Out of theſe ſeven Keyes there is a double* b. *viz. flat and ſharp.* Theſe two Letters in the ſigning are diſtant by the leſſer half Note. So that the regular or dural Scale beginneth in *C.* and the irregular or flat Scale in *F.* b dural is thus marked ♮ and is called *b. quadrate.*

5. *Beſides* b. *molle ,* as they call it , *there is need* of Cancells ✕. *and* cis, dis, fis, *g* is: which are called fict Letters by inſtrumental Muſicians. But *David Moſtart* ſo accommodateth the Muſical Keyes to ſeven new Voices. Four Keyes in the whole are her e

here to be held. The firſt is *C.* in which he will alwayes have *bo* ſung. The ſecond is *G.* five Tones below and four above *G,* he alwayes ſingeth *bo.* The third is *F.* and four above, and five Tones below *F. bo.* is alwayes ſung. Alſo five Notes above *B. molle,* and four under *B. molle,bo.* is alwayes to be ſung. 6. *Muſical Voices are one way rehearſed by the Ancients, and another way by later Muſicians.* The ancient Muſicians did conſtitute theſe ſix *ut, re, mi, fa, ſol, la.* To theſe ſix Voices ſome do add the ſeventh *Si,* left there ſhould be need of ſome Mutation. Concerning this thing *Erycius Puteanus* in his *Muſathena* doth ſo for the moſt part play the Philoſopher. *Guido Aretine* (lived under *Henry* the third Emperour) for his Skill in Muſick among the prime of his Age, and delighted with the perfection of the Senary Number, introduced theſe ſix Syllabic Notes, *ut, re, mi, fa, ſol, la.* which he borrowed and tranſlated out of the Hymne.

Ut *queant laxis* Reſonare fibris ,
MIra geſtorum F Amuli tuorum ,
SOLve pollutum LA bij reatum.

Sancte Johannes.

Theſe ſix Notes ſo invented , do ſhew their uſe every where among Muſicians , but very ſlow and difficult. For what impediment is there of Mutations , confuſion of Keyes , ſubſtitution of Voices? You may ſee moſt (whether with Indignation or no) to have ſpent a good part of their Age upon this Art,

and

and yet to have profited very little , though perfect
many years before in the *Lection* thereof. But the
Difficulty doth hinder,and make it a *remora* to moſt.
Which ſome do thus take away by joyning *ſi.* to
theſe ſix received Notes. For which Note you may
put *Bi.* out of the ſaid Hymne.

Solve polluti la BI. i. reatum.

This therefore ſhall be the order of Notes, *us, re,
mi, fa, ſol, la, bi,* for this *Heptade* theſe following
Reaſons are brought. 1. Whereas Notes are the
Index's of Voyces, and as certain Signs, it is of neceſſity that there ſhould be as many Notes as Voices.
But there are ſeven diſtinct voices ſtabliſhed in that
half verſe *ſeptem diſcrimina vocum.* Therefore there
are ſeven Notes. For by voices are underſtood thoſe
ſeven Sounds, which are diſtinguiſhed by certain Intervalls. Thoſe Intervalls or Diaſtems are called
Tones. Therefore a Sound , and Tone or Intervall
do differ. A Sound is the Voice it ſelf , which being formed by the Mouth , is brought by the Air to
the Ears. A Tone is a Space circumſcribed by two
Sounds : or, the diſtance of a grave and acute Sound:
So that Tones are thoſe Intervals , which are placed
between the firſt and ſecond Sound , the ſecond and
third , the third and fourth , the fourth and fifth ,
the fifth and ſixth , the ſixth and ſeventh. But this
Heptade of Voices , *Ptolomy* in his eleventh Book
concerning Muſick doth confirm ; ſaying , *that by
nature Voices can be made neither more nor fewer then
ſeven.* 2. The *Ægyptians* and *Grecians* have ap-
proved

proved the ſeven *Voyces* by the number of ſeven *Vowells.* For the *Egyptians* as *Demetrius Phalereus* doth teſtifie, did commend their *Gods* by the modulated enunciation of ſeven vowels. And *Plutarch* doth accommodate the *Greeks* ſeven Vowels to ſo many Voices of Muſick. 3. The *Lyre, Cithren,* and certain other muſical Inſtruments which are ſtrung with ſtrings, were anciently of ſeven ſtrings, without doubt, by reaſon of the ſeven Voices. The *Chords* of the *Lyre* were of old in this order, and by theſe Names, *Hypate, Parhypate, Hypermeſe, Meſe, Paramese, Paranete, Nete.* The firſt is called *Hypate,* not only for the acuteneſſe of the Voice, but for a certain excellency and virtue. For *Hypatos* as it were *Hypertatos,* doth ſignifie a degree of Eminency and Dignity. *Nete,* as *Neate,* that is, the laſt or ultimate. Neither have the *Chords* been only by theſe Names, but alſo the Sounds themſelves, nigh this manner. *Hypate* hath to himſelf *Bi.* and ſoundeth acutely: *Parhypate, la,* and doth lullaby: *Hypermeſe, ſol,* and doth ſound ſweetly: *Meſe, fa,* and doth ſound temperately: *Paramese, mi,* and doth delight pleaſantly: *Paranete, re,* and doth grate tremulouſly: *Nete, ut,* and doth, as it were low hoarſly. Furthermore the Ancients did attribute the ſeven *Planets* to ſo many *Chords* of the *Lyre,* in this Order. To *Saturn, Hypate:* to *Jupiter, Parhypate:* to *Mars, Hypermeſe:* to *Sol, Meſe:* to *Venus, Paramese:* to *Mercury, Paranete:* and to *Luna, Nete.* In which Comparation the acuteneſſe and gravity of the *Chords* and *Planets* do reſpond exactly. Although others invert

D 3 the

the order, and attribute to *Saturn* Nete , and to *Lu-na Hypate*. Which Comparation although it may conſiſt : Yet notwithſtanding the firſt is more allowed : becauſe *Saturn* doth proceed in a mundane motion moſt quickly, *Luna* moſt ſlowly. Look *Cicero* in his Dream. From the *Chords* to the Notes we transfer this Comparation , and aſcribe to *Luna*, *vt* ; to *Mercury* , *re* ; to *Venus* , *mi* ; to *ſol* , *fa* ; to *Jupiter* , *la* ; to *Saturn* , *bi*. For ſurely as the *Planet's* do run round the Week , or the Septenary Circle of dayes in their Term or gliding Courſe , and each of them by a certain diurnal viciſſitude of Government do's obtain the primacy : So theſe ſeven Notes do complete the univerſal harmonical *Lection*, divided by *Muſicians* into ſeven Types. Theſe Types are certain and appointed Progreſſions of Notes , diſtinguiſhed by indicial Letters. 4. Theſe ſeven Voices do render all Muſick very facile ; aſwell in the Theory as in the Practiſe , thus. All Muſick is accompliſhed by *Voices*. The Voices being known, Notes are adhibited : To the Notes Characters of Letters ; as appeareth by this *Diagram*.

In a Flat Song.

Between	A B C D E F	and	B C D E F G	alſo	mi fa ſol la bi vt	and	fa ſol la bi vt re	Hemitone Tone Tone Tone Hemitone Tone

In a ſharp Song.

Between		and		alſo		and		
	A		B		la		bi	Tone
	B		C		bi		vt	Hemitone
	C		D		vt		re	Tone
	D		E		re		mi	Tone
	E		F		mi		fa	Hemitone
	F		G		fa		ſol	Tone

Therefore in a Flat Song, *A* hath *mi* conjoyned with it, *B fa*, *C ſol*, *D la*, *E bi*, *F vt*, *G re*. In a ſharp Song, *A* hath *la* aſcribed to it, *B bi*, *C vt*, *D re*, *E mi*, *F fa*, *G ſol*. Which difference the variated Diſpoſition of the *Hemitones* hath begotten. Moreover of theſe Letters only four are expreſſed, *B*, *C*, *F*, *G*. Nor yet thoſe together or conjoynedly, but one or two in the beginning of Lines. The other Letters not noted, you máy know by theſe four. If you aſcend from the *Index Letter*, number the firſt ſeven according to the *Order* of the *Alphabet*, but if you go further, then iterate the ſame: but if you deſcend, proceed by a retrograde *Order*, from the *Line* to the *Intervall*, and from the *Intervall* to the *Line*. Then you may rightly find out the *Letters*; by the *Letters*, the *Notes*; by the *Notes*, the *Voices*; which is the Summe of *Muſick*. Therefore ſee that you be moſt exactly skilled in the aſcending and deſcending *Order* of the *Notes*: and that the *Tones* and *Semitones* being obſerved, you may riſe and fall with your *Voice*. After that, a *Song* being propoſed, you

D 4   may

may paſs from the *Sign* and *Letter* noted , to the
Note anſwering it : from hence , omitting the *Let-*
ters , to the other *Notes.* And this truely is eaſie in a flat *Song* , when *B.* is marked in the begin-
ing of the *Lines,* there it ſheweth that *Fa* is to be
ſung. But in a ſharp Song the difference is of theſe
three Letters , *C. F. G.* of which by that you may
know *Sol,* by that *fa,* laſtly by this *Sol.* Therefore
every where conſult the Signed *Letter* , find out the
Note , and call it by its proper *Voice* , and ſo proceed from thence by aſcending and deſcending : but
if in Singing a *Note* do occur, which hath a peculiar
Letter prefixed , the *Tone* is to be changed, and the
Note of the Letter ſung. Therefore if you have
rightly accommodated the ſeven *Notes* , you may
mixe any Concent , or read any Melody that you
would , whether it be the ſimple *Æolian* , or the
various *Aſian* , or the querulous *Lydian* , or the religious *Phrygian* , or Warlike *Dorian.* But you will
ſay that *Songs* are not concluded in thoſe Seven *Voi-*
ces, but riſe higher. The Anſwer is ready ; As in
numbers when we riſe from the *Monade* to the *De-*
nary, the firſt is the chief of numbers, and by ite-
rating and compounding them we proceed *in infini-*
tum. So in theſe *Voices* after every ſeventh *Sound* ,
it returneth to the firſt , but more ſubtile ; and after
every ſeventh *Note* the firſt : and ſo alſo afterward
the ſecond of *Notes* doth agree with the ninth ; the
third , with the tenth ; the fourth,with the eleventh;
the fifth , with the twelfth ; the ſixth , with the
thirteenth; the ſeventh , with the fourteenth , *&c.*
Of *Sounds* there is the ſame Judgement. From a
Muſical

Muſical Inſtrument, which by way of Eminency is ſo called, you may take the Experience of your Ears. But in theſe *Notes* obſerve a double order of *Intenſion* and *Remiſſion*. *Intenſion* (by the *Greeks* E-*pitaſis*) is the commotion of the *Voice*, from the graver place to an acute: *Remiſſion* (by the *Greeks* *Aneſis*) from an acuter to a grave. But it is worth the pains, that here ſome Director or Ruler of the *Voice* (as *Tertullian* ſpeaks) go before and lead. Hitherto *Puteanus*, with whom worketh *David Mo-ſtart in his Introduction of Muſick*, as indeed he proveth the Septenary of *Voices*. But he doth ſub-ſtitute other *Voices* in this manner, *bo, ce, di, ga, lo, ma, ni.* But ſo that in *C* of a ſharp Song *bo* is ſung. Alſo in *F.* of a flat, *bo. e. gr.*

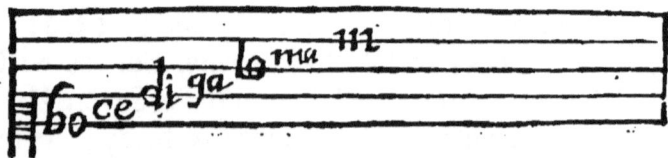

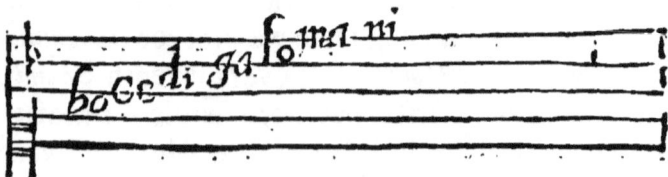

But let *Moſtart* himſelf be heard. bo ſaith thus, *It is worth our labour ſeriouſly to* t *ſuch Muſical Voices as exhibite unto us a perfect Octave,*

ſo

ſo that it be the Conſequence of eight Tones or Notes: by which Connexion and Series the perfection of any *Melody may be performed*, without any Mutation: which indeed is the torture of tender wits. And the Series is this, *bo, ce, di, ga, lo, ma, ni. bo* Which Abridgement if it ſhould be admitted, thoſe old vulgar Keyes ſhould be aboliſhed, the Letters of thoſe ſeven Syllables being only retained in every Song, *viz. b. c. d. g. l. m. n.*

For Example ſake.

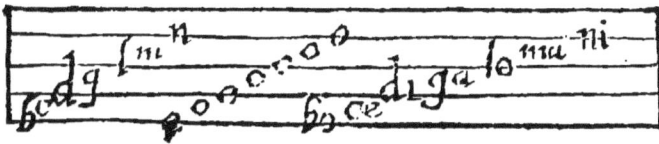

Therefore *Moſtart* rejeſteth the ſix *Voices* of the Ancients; becauſe they complete not an *Octave*, and for that Cauſe require *Mutation*, which is the torture of the Ingenious: and alſo the ſeven *Voices* of latter *Muſicians*, becauſe they do not reſpond to the ſeven *Letters* or *Keyes*. But becauſe thoſe *Voices* of the *Ancients* be much uſed in *Schools*, therefore let us ſee their uſe. For 1. Some of thoſe *Voices* are ſuperiour, by which a Song deſcendeth, *viz. la, ſol, fa*, and others are inferiour, by which it aſcendeth, *ut, re, mi*. 2. All thoſe *Voices* are equally diſtant from another by a *Tone*, beſides *mi* and *fa* which are diſtant by a *Semitone*. 3. Of theſe
Voices,

Voices, *vt* and *fa* ſound flatly ; *mi* and *la* ſharply ; the reſt, meanly. But concerning this thing others ſpeaks thus, *vt* and *ſol* denote Sweetneſſe , *re* and *la* gravity, *mi* Lamentation, *fa* threatnings. Laſtly , others conſider theſe *Voices* thus. *Vt* and *fa* are flat *Voices* by *b moll* , becauſe they emit a flat and effeminate Sound : *re* and *la* natural , becauſe they afford a natural and middle Sound: *mi* and *la b* durales , becauſe they make a ſharp and manlike Sound. According to theſe Verſes ;

Vt *cum* fa *mollis vox eſt* ; *quia Cantica mollit* :
Mi *cum* la *dura eſt,   Nam duras efficit odas.*
Sol *naturalis (quoniam neutras facit) & re.*

4. *Certain Voices do anſwer all Keyes.* Thus

A	*la*	*mi*	*re*
B	*fa*	*mi*	
C	*ſol*	*.fa*	*vt*
D	*la*	*ſol*	*re*
E	*la*	*mi*	
F	*fa*	*vt*	
G	*ſol*	*re*	*vt*

5. Theſe *Voices* are circumſcribed in certain parallel Lines, ſo that in a Song we may aſcend and deſcend ; and that in a progreſſion either continued, or diſcontinued. Continued Progreſſion is that which obſerveth the natural Order of *Voices*, and is called a natural Song ; As ,

Diſcon-

Diſcontinued Progreſſion is the Mutation of a *Voice* , which is conſidered either in the minor or greater *Syſtem*. *Mutation* in the leſſer *Syſtem* , is made for the Paucity of *Voices :* and it is either *Vocal* or mental. That is called *explicite*, this *implicite*. And both is diverſe in a flat Song, and in a ſharp. In a flat Song *Mutation* is made in *d. a. g.* whoſe memo‑ rial Note is *dag*. In a ſharp Song *Mutation* is made in *d. a. e.* Whoſe *Voice* of remembrance is *dea*. In the greater *Syſtem* Mutation is made according to the *triple Scale*, The firſt is *b dural Scale*; which is the Progreſſion of Muſical *Voices*, riſing from *a.* into *b.* ſharply, that is, by the *Voice mi*. The ſecond is *d moll* ; which is the progreſſion of Muſical *Voices*, riſing from *a.* into *b moll* , that is the *Voice fa*. The third is the fict *Scale*, which in every *Key* admit‑ teth a range *Voice*. And hence it is called *fict Mu‑ ſick:* becauſe modulated by feigned Voices. *i. e.* by ſuch as are ſung in any Key, in which eſſentially they are not contained. As *vt* in *e. re.* in *f.* and ſo on.

This

This is the Type of the *Triple Scale*.

Tetrachord	Note	b							
5.Tetrachord	ee	b							*la*
	dd							*la*	*ſol*
	cc							*ſol*	*fa*
	bb							*fa*	*mi*
4.Tetrachord of excellents.	aa	b					*la*	*mi*	*re*
	g						*ſol*	*re*	*vt*
	f						*fa*	*vt*	
	e	b				*la*	*mi*		
3.Tetrachord of Superiors.	d				*la*	*ſol*	*re*		
	c				*ſol*	*fa*	*vt*		
	b	b			*fa*	*mi*			
	a			*la*	*mi*	*re*			
2.Tetrachord of Finals.	G			*ſol*	*re*	*vt*			
	F			*fa*	*vt*				
	E	b	*la*	*mi*					
	D		*ſol*	*re*					
1.Tetrachord of grave Sounds.	C		*fa*	*vt*					
	B	b	*mi*						
	A	b	*re*						
	Γ		*vt*						

And this is the old *Diaton* Scale. Thus we have contracted the new *Syntonian* Scale of *Lippius*.

96	90 16		1 2 3 4 5 6 7 8 9 10 11 12 13
120	108	11	
144	135	10	
180	160	8 bb	
220	192		
270	240 6 f		
320	288 5		
384	360 4 b		
480	432	3 ſ	
576	540		
720	640 2 B		
864	768		
1080	960		
1280	1152		
	1440 1		

In this Table muſical *Sounds* are ſo contained, that
firſt there is the *Simple Uniſon.*   2. The *Tonus minor.*   3. The *Tonus major.*   4. The *greater Semitone.*   5. The *Semiditone.* 6. The *Ditone.*   7. The
Fourth.   8. The *Fifth.*   9. The *leſſer Sixth.* 10.
The *greater Sixth.*   11. The *leſſer Seventh.*   12.
The *greater Seventh.*   13. The *Octave.* And this
is the *Cyclus* or Compaſs of the *Diapaſon.* Concerning the Proportions of all theſe *Sounds*, look
into the former *Chap.* thus *v gr.* To the *Octave* aſcribe
1. 2. to the *Septima* 8. 15. and ſo of others: So
that the leſſer number be applied to the upper Note
in the *Scale.* The ſignificates of the Letters. *B. L.*
b,l,bb. are a little before called *bo.ce.di.ga.lo.ma.ni.*

✛✛✛✛✛✛✛✛✛✛✛✛✛✛✛✛✛✛✛✛✛✛✛

Chap. VI.

Of the Muſical DYAS.

Precepts.

HItherto of the ſimple part of an harmonical Song: the compounded
part thereof followeth; whoſe tractation is called practical or Melopoetical
Muſick, if the form of the Song be added.
The compounded part of an harmonical

cal Song, is that which ariſeth from muſical ſounds or Monads conjoyned accoꝛding to thꝛee Dimenſions.

And it is either pꝛimary oꝛ ſecondary.

The pꝛimary is called harmony and conſonancy, which doth ariſe from graue and acute ſounds united by ſuch a pꝛopoꝛtion, that it may delight the hearing.

The ſecondary is diſſonancy oꝛ Anarmoſty, which ariſeth from ſuch a pꝛopoꝛtion of graue and acute Sounds, that it offendeth the hearing.

And this double part is either a muſical Dyas, oꝛ Tryas, of which the one is perfect, and the other imperfect.

A muſical Dyas, is that which ariſeth from two ſounds : conſonant and harmonical from Conſonants, and diſſonant from Diſſonants.

And it is moꝛe ſimple, oꝛ moꝛe compounded. That is called radical, this radicated.

The ſimple Conſonant Dyads, are ſeuen; viz. An Octave, Fifth, Fourth, Ditone, Semiditone, greater Sixth, and leſſer Sixth: the diſſonant Dyads are the other ſimple Interualls, as the Tone major and minor, the Semitone greater and leſſer, the Seventh greater and leſſer ; and laſtly , all ſimple Interballs not Juſt , as the Semioctave , Semififth, *&c.*

The Dyas moze compounded is that which ariſeth from the ſimple Dyas : and that again is either conſonant oz Diſſonant : and both compounded either once , twice , thzice, oz ſo fozward. In Dyads once compounded the Double Octave , alſo the Octave with a Fifth , the Octave with a Fourth , and Octave with a Ditone Do conſonate:but the Octave with both tones, with a Semitone , and with an Intervall not juſt doth Diſſonate. In Dyads twice compounded the triple Octave, and Double Octave , with a Fifth Do conſonate : but the Double Octave with both tones , with the Semitone , and ſo fozwards ; Doth Diſſonate.

R u l e s.

1. *There are two Arbiters of congruous and incongruous Proportions.*

The firſt is *ſuperior,* which doth judge of Proportions

tions *à priori*, to wit, *Logos*: the other is *inferior*, which doth exactly judge of Sounds *à poſteriori*, to wit, the *Hearing*. And there is a neceſſity that both theſe Judges ſhould concur, as *Ptolomy* doth rightly teach: but falſly *Pythagoras*, who doth think that nothing here is to be attributed to the hearing; and falſly *Ariſtoxenus*, that ſuppoſeth nothing here is to be attributed to *Ration*. But the nature of Proportions is demonſtrated by the *Monochord*: for that in it all Muſical *Diaſtems* are contained.

2. *The Simple Uniſon is the Radix of all Conſonancy and Diſſonancy.*

Vulgarly they imagine that the Uniſon doth both conſonate and diſſonate. But they erre; for the *Uniſon* doth equiſonate only, becauſe it hath the proportion of Equality, and is the principal of every Interval. *e. gr.*

Rightly therefore the ſimple *Uniſon* is made the *Radix* of *Conſonancy* and *Diſſonancy*.

3. *The*

3. *The Simple Consonant Dyads are in number Seven, and may be called Simple Concordancies.*

Vulgarly they thus rehearse the Simple *Concordancies.* There are twelve *Concordancies*, the 1. 3. 5. 6. 8. 10. 12. 13. 15. 17. 19. 20. And these are divided two wayes. First, there are Simple, replicated or triplicated. The *Simple Concordances* are the 1. 3. 5. 6. which are also called primary. The Replicated are such as are equisonant to the former, conceived by a double Dimension, as the 8. 10. 12. 13. Otherwise called Secondary. For in Sound the *Octave* doth associate with the *Unison*, the *tenth* with the *third*, the *twelfth* with the *fifth*, and the *thirteenth* with the *sixth*. The *triplicated Consonants* are the 15. 17. 19. 20. otherwise called *tertiaries.* Of these the 15. is coequated in Sound with the *Octave* and the *first*: the *seventeenth* with the *tenth* and *third*, and the *nineteenth* with the *twelfth* and *fifth*, and the *twentieth* doth equisonate with the *thirteenth* and *sixth*, According to this Type.

1. 3. 5. 6.
8. 10. 12. 13.
15. 17. 19. 20.

Lastly, There are *Concordances* perfect, or imperfect. The *Perfect* are those which can stand by themselves, that is, begin and terminate a Song: as
the

the 1. 5. 8. The _imperfeƈt_ are thoſe which may concur in _Counterpoint_, as the 3. 6. 10. The _Diſcordan-
ces_ are nine, _viz._ the 2. 4. 7. 9. 11. 14. 16. 18. 21.
Others alſo do number the _perfeƈt_ _Concordances_ thus,
the 1. 3. 5. 8. becauſe they reſpond to the _Pythogori-
cal_ _Quaterñary_. But it behoveth them to play the Philoſophers of _Concordances_ more acurately. There are
ſeven _Concordances_ or ſimple _Conſonances._ Of which
the _Oƈtave_ is the firſt, which is of a _dupla_ proportion between 2. and 1. In his Terms the moſt ſimple Conveniency is diverſe, as is between the whole
and the half. The _Fifth_ doth obtain the ſecond place;
then followeth the _fourth_; then the _Ditone_ or _third_
in a ſharp Song; then the _Semiditonus_, which is the
third in a flat Song; in the laſt place ſave one is the
Sexta major in a ſharp Song; and in the laſt place,
the _Sexta minor_ in a flat Song. And this is the Order of _Perfeƈtion._ For although every Simple _Con-
ſonancy_ is perfeƈt in his degree; yet notwithſtanding
in reſpeƈt of another, it is either more perfeƈt or
imperfeƈt; yet ſo as the firſt and moſt perfeƈt is the
Oƈtave, that compounded _Uniſon_; the moſt imperfeƈt and laſt, is the leſſer _Sixth_; the intermediate
are meaſurably as the moſt perfeƈt or moſt imperfeƈt
are nearer. Here _Muſicians_ do wonder, why the
Septinary begetteth no _Conſonancy_, when as it num-
bereth all ſimple _Conſonances_. And this is the _Scheme_
of thoſe ſeven ſimple _Conſonances._

Of theſe the firſt three are perfect, the four latter are imperfect. And indeed principally the *Octave*, in reſpect of his excellent perfection doth *equiſonate* and *uniſonate* after the *Uniſon* and ſimple *Equiſon*. After it the *Fifth* for its perfection doth conſonate by his moſt grateful, firm, and maſculine Sound. After it the *Ditone* or greater *Third* by his ſweet Imperfection doth concent but more cheerfully, ſtrongly, and lively. Then the *Semiditone* or leſſer *Third* alſo by his ſweet Imperfection doth concent more ſoftly, remiſly, and heavily. Then the greater *Sixth* by his Imperfection doth circumſonate as it were more high and pleaſantly. Laſt of all the leſſer *Sixth* doth alſo ſo circumſonate but more ſlowly, flatly, and weakly. Theſe four latter *Conſonances* were not uſed by the *Ancients* in their *Diatone Scale:* but now they are uſed moſt chiefly, naturally, and artificially in the *Syntonian Scale*. And this is the Order of Perfection in the ſeven ſimple *Conſonances*. The Order of the Craſſitude of Sound, or of Intenſion and Remiſſion is this, which is firmly contrary to the firſt. After the ſimple *Uniſon* is the *Semiditone*, then the *Ditone*, then the *Fourth*, *Fifth*, *Sixth minor*, *Sixth major*, and *Octave*. From theſe it is an eaſie thing to Judge of *Simple Diſſonances*, to wit, becauſe they are all *Tones* placed without the *Septinary* of *Conſonances*; as the greater and leſſer *Tone*; the greater and leſſer *Semitone*; the greater and leſſer *Seventh*, and laſtly *Intervalls* not juſt deficient. For in theſe are diſagreeing Proportions, whoſe extreme Sounds do but ill agree, and therefore if they be put together, they offend the Ear.

4. *Com-*

4. *Compounded Dyads do imitate the nature of Simple.*

This is true both of compounded *Concordances* and *Diſcordances*, according to that elegant *Axiom* of *Muſicians.* *Of Octaves there is the ſame and like Judgement.* And that for the eſſential Similitude of *dupla*, *quadrupla*, *octupla*, and *ſedecupla* Proportion, as 16. 8. 4. 2. 1. Alſo of compounded *Dyads* the *Order* of perfection and Craſſitude, is like unto the *Order* of their ſimple *Dyads.* Otherwiſe although the Compoſition of perfect *Concordances* might proceed *in infinitum :* yet notwithſtanding becauſe they are not the ſame Terms of *Sound* and *Hearing* (which thing therefore obtaineth in the reſt of the *Senſes)* it is neceſſary that we be mindful of Medioerity, leſt we create trouble to the Eare, by any Sound too great or too acute.

5. *It behoveth us alwayes to have in our Eye the Radixes of Simple Dyads.*

As it is very compendious, to obſerve ſimple only and radical *Dyads* both conſonant and diſſonant, and then by thoſe to judge of compounded *Dyads :* ſo alſo it is very compendious to conſider the Roots of thoſe ſimple *Dyads*, according to this Type.

Ba.

Bo.	ni.	ma.	lo.	ga.	di.	ce.
90.	96.	108.	120.	135.	144.	160.
1.2.4.8.				3.6.		5.

See before in the *Syntonic Table*. Here, between the *Consonances* of the *Octave* and *fourth*, the *Radix* is the *Fifth :* of both *Sixes* , both *Thirds*. Therefore the *Octave* and *fourth* may be reduced to the *Fifth* ; and the *sixth* to the *third*. The Root of simple Dissonant *Dyads* is the second, to which both *Sevenths* may be reduced.

✠✠✠✠✠✠✠✠✠✠✠✠✠✠✠✠✠✠✠✠✠✠✠

CHAP. VII.

Of the Musical TRIAS.

PRECEPTS.

THE Musical Trias is that which doth arise from three sounds and as many Dyads : otherwise called the unitri-sonous Radix.

And it is either consonant or dissonant.

The consonant Trias is that in which a third and a fifth doth concur, yet so as

E 4   that

that it ariſeth from **two** thirds.
The **diſſonant** Tryas **is that which ariſeth from** ſeconds.

.

RULES.

1. *The Harmonical* Tryas *is the Root of all the Harmony that can be invented,*

And may be called the *unitriſonous Radix :* becauſe it doth conſiſt of three *Monads* or *Sounds*, and as many *Dyads :* all of them in that whole *Tryas* , and every one moſt ſweetly concenting one with another, becauſe they are joyned together in a certain Order by juſt Proportions. Thoſe *Sounds* or *Monads* being three in number, and as many *Dyads*, making this *Trias*, are theſe. Firſt , the two *Extremes* are diſtant one from another by a *Diapente* , which is of a *Seſquialtera* Proportion. Then there is one middle , which by his ſofter ſweetneſſe doth joyn thoſe two Extremes, concenting together by a perfect and maſculine *Sound*, and is diſtant from one of them by a *Ditone* , and from the other by a *Semiditone*. There is the Proportion of a *Seſquiquarta*, here of a *Seſquiquinta. e. gr.*

Here

Here 4. and 5. then 4. and 6. then laſtly 5. and 6.
do conſpire. This *unitriſonous Radix* is the Rule
and Meaſure of all *Conſonances*, and is alwayes in
one manner. Yet this only is the difference, that
in a flat *Song* it is more *imperfect* and *ſoft*, but in a
ſharp *Song*, more *natural*, *perfect*, *nobler*, and
ſweet. The firſt hath the *Ditone* above the *Semiditone*, the latter hath the *Ditone* beneath the *Semiditone*. Moreover this *Radix* is either increaſed or
diffuſed. The increaſed, is that which hath the
Octave for his Companion, to excite the more various and fuller *Harmony*. The diffuſed is that, whoſe
radical *parts* or *voices* are not ſo near unto one another, becauſe diſperſed into various *Octaves*. For the
nearer the *Voices* are one to another, the more excellent is the *Symphony*. The beſt Diſpoſition of
all look above *Chap. 5. Rule 6.* where I do write of
ſigned *Keyes*.

2. *The Muſical* Trias *doth ariſe both from Arithmetical and Geometrical Proportion.*

Proportion is threefold: Firſt *arithmetical*, which
is,

is, when the *numbers* are diſtant one from another
by an equal Difference, and that either continued;
as 1. 2. 3. 4. or diſ-joyned, as 3. 6. 8. 11. There
the *Difference* is an *unity*, here a *ternary*. Secondly,
Geometrical; which is, when there is the ſame *Ration* of more *Terms* compared with one another:
and it is either continued, as 4. 8. 16. or diſ-joyned, as 2. 4. 8. 16. Thirdly, *muſical* or *harmonical* Proportion, ariſeth from *arithmetical* and *geometrical:* and it is no other, then a *Symmetry* of
Concents, which is diſcerned in the moſt perfect muſical *Triade*; which *Lippius* therefore calleth the
chiefeſt, ſweeteſt, and plaineſt (*ompendium of Me-
lopœtical* (*Muſick*. But let us purſue theſe things
further. Muſical or Harmonical Proportion is the
Symetry or Equality of *Concents*, which doth ariſe from
Proportion *arithmetical* and *geometrical*; ſo that
three Terms being put, even as the greateſt is to
the leaſt, ſo is the Difference of the middle, and
the greateſt to the Difference of the middle and
leaſt. As 3. 4. 6. Here, as *Six* are the *Duplum* to
three: ſo two (which is the Difference between
4. and 6.) are the *Duplum* to the Unity, which is
the Difference between 3. and 4. Such is the proportion in the *unitriſonus Radix*. 1. 3. 5. Alſo between 6. 8. 12. For three Terms muſically proportional are found from three arithmetically proportional, if the firſt arithmetically proportional be
multiplied into the *ſecond* and *third*, and the *ſecond*
into the *third*. So from theſe three *arithmetically*
proportional 2. 4. 6. are found theſe three muſically
proportional. 8. 12. 24. But that numbers are muſically

ſically proportional , is hence manifeſt , if in them
thoſe three Proportions are found , on which all
Muſick doth depend : to wit , *Dupla* , or *Diapaſon* , which doth conſtitute an *Octave : Seſquialtera* ,
or *Diapente* , which doth conſtitute a *Fifth :* and
Seſquitertia, or *Diateſſaron* , which doth conſtitute
a *Fourth.* So in theſe Numbers 6. 4. 3. between 6.
and 3. is *dupla :* between 6. and 4. *ſeſquialtera :* between 4. and 3. *ſeſquitertia.* I ſay , *three* to *four* ,
are in the *ſeſquitertian Ration* , as the *Diateſſaron
Syſtem : four* to *ſix* are in the *Seſquialtera Ration*, as
the *Diapente : three* to *ſix* are in the *dupla Ration* , as
the *Diapaſon Syſtem.* And of theſe the reſt are compounded , *viz.* the *Diſdiapaſon, &c.* This alſo is of
force in *Organical Muſick.* For if two Strings e-
qually thick and ſtretched differ in Longitude by a
Seſquialtera Ration, benig ſtruck, they will equally
Sound the Harmony of a *Diapente :* if they differ
in Longitude by a *Seſquitertia Ration*, a *Diateſſaron :*
if by a *dupla* , a *Diapaſon*, which vulgarly they call
an *Octave* , as a *Diapente* a *fifth* , and a *Diateſſaron*
a *Fourth.* The ſame is in Hollowneſſe , or in
Whiſtles. From this Operation alwayes except the
unitriſonous Radix, becauſe it is the foundation of o-
ther muſical proportions.

CHAP.

✠⊕✠

Chap. VIII.

Of the Forme of an Harmonical Song.

Precepts.

THus much concerning the matter of
an harmonical Song : now of the
forme thereof, which is the artificial
disposition of Musical Monads, Dyads, and
Tryads, according to the Text, and this
is called Melodie.

Melodie is simple, or compounded.
That is called Monodie, this Symphony.

Simple Melodie is that which is content
with one onely Series of musical voices:
as is discerned in Choral Musick, called
Unicinium.

Compounded Melodie is that which
doth conjoyne more simple Melodies between themselves : and is usually called
Counterpoint; as is discerned in figural
Musick.

Muſick. To which appertaine Songs of two, three, and four voices, &c.

Counterpoint is either ſimple or coloured.

Simple Counterpoint is that which hath leaſt of Artifice : and may be called pure Compoſition, whoſe Rules or Ornaments are the Sounds of Longitude, Latitude, or Craſſitude.

Counterpoint coloured is that which hath more of Art : and may be called adorned Compoſition, whoſe Rules or Ornaments do reſpect the Longitude, Latitude, and Craſſitude of a Sound.

Rules.

1. *A Muſical Text doth give as it were a Soul to an Harmonical Song, as to the Image thereof.*

Wherefore ſeeing the *Image* is ſuch as is the *Archetype*, the practical *Muſician* or *Compoſer* as they call him, is to take care that he underſtand aright the nature of his Text, in reſpect of things and words. For an Harmonical Song ought to be accommodated both to things and words. The things may be all divine

vine and humane matters, but chiefly practical, which
concern the active felicity of man; the mean to ac-
quire which, is virtue moderating the Affections,
which do depend upon things or objects either great,
or low, or mean: and thoſe again either pleaſant or
delightful, or unpleaſant and ſorrowful, or moderate. Words may be either of proſe or verſe, yet
ſo as that they be like unto things practical, even,
and congruous. So that he ought to know the nature
of all Letters, (of which in my *Rhetoricks.*)
Moreover, an harmonical *Song* will rightly expreſs
the *Text*, if the Muſician give heed to the *trine Dimenſion* of *Sound*, viz. *Longitude*, *Latitude*, and
Craſſitude. For things grave are rightly expreſſed
by long and profound Sounds: light things by ſhort
and acute Sounds: Maſculine things by ſharp Sounds:
ſoft things by flat Sounds: pleaſant things by lively
and quick Sounds: Sad things by languid and ſlow
Sounds: and mean things by mean Sounds; as we
ſee it falleth out in Poeſy.

2. *More Simple Me,lody, which is called Monadie, is firſt to be compoſed.*

A young Compoſer ſhould firſt compoſe the moſt
ſimple Melodies, which ariſe not from Muſical *Dyads* and *Tryads*, but from *Monads*, or a ſimple
Diſpoſition of muſical Voices. *e. gr.* Let this be
the Subject, *Laudate Dominum*, which may be ſung
with this Melodie.

Or

Or after the new manner , which *Lippius* hath ,
which dependeth upon the *Syntonick* Table, in the 5
Chapter before mentioned.

288. 320. 288. 270. 270. 288.
Lau - da - - - te - - do - - mi - num.
2. $1\frac{1}{2}$ $\frac{9}{2}$ $\frac{1}{2}$ $\frac{2}{3}$ $\frac{1}{2}$ 2.

Here the Numbers placed above the Text do ſhew
the *Notes* of the *Syntonic* Table : and the numbers
underneath do expreſſe the meaſure of the Touch.
Therefore ſuch will be the Series according to this
new Mode.

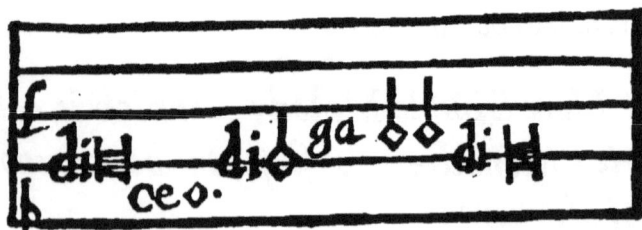

3. *Compounded Melodie doth reſpeƈt ei-*
ther two, three, or four Simple Me-
lodies , cardinal and radical.

Of theſe the Compoſition and Connexion of four
Me-

lodies is moſt perfeᶜt.   For as a body mixed of four
Elements, is a temperament of four humours : So
every harmonical *Polyphony* doth ariſe from four ſimple Melodies.   Of theſe two are extreme, the *Baſs*
which is the graveſt ; and the *Diſcantus* which is the
acuteſt : and two are intermediate ; the one is nearer
to the *Baſs*, which is the *Tenor* ; and the other is
nearer to the *Diſcantus*, which is the *Altus*, according to the Diſpoſition of the four Elements, *Earth,*
Water, Air, and *Fire.*   Of which, two are extreme,
and as many *Median,* as is noted in our *Phyſicks.*
And this is the Muſical *Tetras*, in which the Melody
of the *Baſs* is fundamental, whence its name is from
Baſis a foundation : or *Baſſus* profound : the Melodie of the *Tenor* and *Diſcantus* (whoſe viciſſitude is
very elegant) is principal or regal.   Laſtly the Melodie of the *Altus* is explemental.   This *Tetras*, or
Song of four voices, doth comprehend both muſical *Monads, Dyads,* and *Tryads,* aſwell Simple as
Compounded, and is the *Radix* of all perfeᶜt Muſical Compoſition.   This therefore is the Order in
Muſicks.   The Muſical *Monade* is the *Radix* of one
Melodie, or Song of one Voice : the *Dyas* of two:
the *Trias* of three : and the *Tetras* of four : Moreover this Compoſition is called Counterpoint, becauſe point is put againſt point.

4. *Pure Compoſition, or Simple Coun-*
terpoint ; hath this Artifice.

   1. Pure Compoſition doth make the four *Melo-*

lodies, more ſimple, plain, and eaſie : yet ſo that it keepeth the *trine Dimenſion* of Sound. 2. *This is the Rule of the Longitude of a Sound.* Every one of the four *radical Melodies* doth ſo proceed by his *Monads*, that Notes of more ſimple value may be added, the *Touch* being every where equal. 3. The Rules of Latitude is this. 1. All the members of all the *Melodies* do make a *Conſonancy* ; which doth depend upon that *unitroſonous harmonical Radix* , of which mention is made in the foregoing Chapter. And becauſe the parts and productions of that *Triade* are various, the *Conſonancys* may be mingled among themſelves, yet ſo as that the peculiar *Ration* of the perfecter of them be kept : for in every *Genus* that which is moſt perfect is the meaſure of the reſt. 2. All melodies ſhould be compared with themſelves moſt diligently. *viz.* The *Baſſ* with the *Tenor*, the *Tenor* with the *Altus*, the *Altus* with the *Diſcantus* , the *Baſſ* with the *Altus*, the *Tenor* with the *Diſcantus* , laſtly, the *Baſſ* with the *Diſcantus*. Or more briefly, the *Tenor* with the *Baſſ*, the *Altus* with the *Tenor* and *Baſs*, the *Diſcantus* with the *Altus* , *Tenor*, and *Baſs*. For ſo every one compared with another will make ſix times an excellent Song of two Parts : So that every part of the *Melody* will be adorned with ſome harmonical *Dyade*. And alſo in thoſe *Dyades*, varietie is to be uſed, yet ſo that the perfecter do rule. 3. *Conſonant Dyades* by aſcending and deſcending together may all mutually *antecede* and follow one another , if they be of divers *ſpecies* : but if of the ſame, as the three perfect *Conſonancies* with the ſimple *unison* , they may

not,

not, but the other imperfect *Dyads* may. But more
briefly, two ſimple *Uniſons* may not be put together aſcending or deſcending : nor two *Octaves*, nor
two *Fifths*, nor two *Fourths*. 4. *Thoſe Dyads
which are nearer in Craſſitude, will better precede and
ſucceed, then thoſe which are more remote.* To
which purpoſe is that ſaying of *Muſicians, By how
much nearer Voices are to one another, by ſo much they
make the better Symphony.* 5. *Monads ſhould be
applied ſo in all Melodies, that every one ſhould elegantly walk in his own Region*, and commonly of
one *Octave*, or *Diapaſon*. 6. *Let the Baſs always
take the lower part or foundation of the harmonical
Triade in the place of the graveſt : but the Tenor in
the place of the graver, the Altus of the acuter, and
the Diſcantus of acuteſt Monads :* So let them take
all three parts of the harmonical *Triade*, *viz.* The
loweſt or firſt, the middle and laſt. But in augmentation and multiplication the firſt of the *Triade*
is chiefly to be repeated, the laſt more rarely, the
middle ſeldomeſt. 7. *Let Melodies aſſociate by
gradual, not by skipping motion.* For if every
Melodie do proceed rather by degrees, then flie vi-
olently by greater *Intervalls* and *Leaps*, it will be
more grateful to the Ears; yet the *Baſs* is allowed to
move by Leaps. 8. *Let the Baſs be firſt compoſed.*
Becauſe it is the foundation of the *Triads*. Here-
to belongeth this Rule. Better is that harmonical
Triade whoſe *Baſis* is loweſt, then thoſe whoſe *Baſis* is in an higher place. But now let us ſee an Example. Let the Text be *Laudate Dominum.* And
this you may thus expreſs in a pure Song. Go to the
Syntonian

Syntonian Table , and from thence pick out Conſo-
nanciesafter this manner.

	2.	1½ ½		½ ½	2.
Diſcantus.	180	192 180	180 180	180.
Altus.	240	240 240	216 216	240.
Tenor.	288	320 288	270 270	288.
Baſſus.	360	480 360	540 540	720.

Lau --da --te -- do -- mi -- num.

*Theſe Conſonancies you may thus transfer into the
great Syſtem.*

Lau - da - te - - do-mi-num.

Or if you had rather you may thus write the ſeveral * Touches in ſeveral Cells.

*Touch is that which *Muſicians* call *Tactus*,
or the *ſtroke* of the hand bywhich Time is meaſured.
Or it is the ſucceſſive Motion of the hand , direct-
ing by equal meaſure the Quantity of all *Notes* and
Pauſes in a Song, according to the variety of *Signes*
and *Proportions.* The parts thereof are Elevation
and Depreſſion ; or the Fall and Riſe of the hand.

Be- -ne-dic- -a--ni-ma-me-a-Je-ho--va.

In the latter Example you may obſerve the *Tenor* to have the ſame Voice with the *Baſs* in the firſt Cell : and in the Sixth and Seventh, two *Minums* put for one *Semibreve.*

V. *Adorned Compoſition, or Coloured Counterpoint, is contained in theſe Rules.*

1. *Adorned* Compoſition doth conſtitute a Song harmonical more *broken, florid,* and *coloured,* therefore more difficult and effectual. Therefore this doth as it were *garniſh* theſe three Dimenſions of a Song with various *Gems* and *flowers :* ſo that pure Compoſition may rightly be compared to *Grammer,* which teacheth to ſpeak purely : and adorned Compoſition to *Rhetorick,* which teacheth to ſpeak Elegantly. 2. *Artificial Licenſes* are uſed in adorned Compoſition. For as there are allowed Poetical Lic enſes,

Licenſes, which do beautifie *Art*, and not deſtroy
it: ſo alſo there are *Melopoetical* Licenſes, by which
the pure and ſimple Dimenſions of a Song are beau-
tified. 3. Theſe are the Ornaments of *Longitude*.
1. An *harmonical* Song is adorned with the varietie of a *Spondaic*, and *trochaic* Touch: and of unequal Notes, eſpecially *Syncopated*. So the *Baſs*
doth move more ſlowly, and the other Melodies with coloured *celeritie*; which is that in Muſick, as flouriſhing is in Writing. 2. An harmonical Song according to the Nature of the Text,
is diſtinguiſhed by *Reſts* and *Cloſes*. For even
as Speech is diſtinguiſhed by *Comma's, Colons*, and
due *Periods*; ſo ought an harmonical Song, according to the nature of the Text, to be diſtinguiſhed
by greater and leſſer *Reſts*; alſo by *Cloſes native*,
primarie, *ſecondarie*, *tertiarie*, *peregrine*, more
perfeſt, or more imperfeſt. A perfeſt Cloſe doth
conſiſt of three *Voiees*; the *antepenult, penult*, and
laſt: by which the *Cloſe* is chiefly known, and which
is to ariſe out of an harmonical *Triade*. *e. g.*

The *Primarie Cloſe* is that whoſe laſt is the firſt;
the *ſecondary*, the *ſupreme*; the *tertiarie* the middle
of the *Triade*; but of theſe in the following Chapter. 4. The *Ornaments* of *Latitude* are theſe. An
harmonical Song ſhould be ſo expreſſed by *Voice* or
Inſtrument, or both together; that according to the
Co1-

Condition of the Text, an aſperous, ſharp, ſwift, full, gentle, flat, ſubmiſs, or ſmall Spirit, &c. ſhould be heard. 5. The *Ornaments* of *Craſſitude* have theſe *Axioms*. 1. *Varietie* ſhould chiefly rule in an harmonical Song; I ſay varietie of *Dyad's* and *Triads*, more grave, more mean, more acute, ſimple and compounded, diffuſed and augmented, more perfect, and more imperfect, natural and fict. Hence is a various Licence: for in the *Baſs* it is lawful to uſe the laſt and middle *Monade* of an *Unitriſonous Radix*: and *Dyads* prohibited, may antecede and follow one another; and a *Dias* and a *Trias* alſo *anarmonical* may be uſed. All which things are done either covertly or openly. Covertly, either by greater *Reſts*, or by Sounds not offending by reaſon of their ſwiftneſſe, or by contrary made Sounds; or by an excuſeing *Polyphonie*, or by *Syncope*. Openly for the texts ſake, and ſingular Artifice. *v. gr.* If the Text command, and as it were compel to maniſeſt ſome Diſcord. According to that of the *Logicians*; Contraries placed nigh themſelves are the more clearly illuſtrated. When therefore in Singing ſome harſh ſound is heard, which preſently paſſeth into a ſweet harmony, the hearing is therewith more affected, than if there were a current of perpetual Harmony. 2. When the whole harmonical Song is rendred more beautiful by the ornament of *Celerity* and *Syncope*; then chiefly the *Cloſe* ſhould be artificial. 3. *Polyphony* or multiplication of *cardinal melodies* do very much adorn Singing. *e. gr.* As if there be two, three, or more *Baſſes*, *Tenor's*, *Altus's*, *Diſcant's*, and

and thoſe placed in certain *Quires*, according to
the Text and Circumſtances. 4. The various manner and motion of *aſcending* and *deſcending*, is
granted to principle Melodies and ſometimes out of
their Proper Regions; as for the *Baſs* to invade the
Confines of the *Tenor*, or the *Tenor* of the *Altus*.
5. The ornament of muſical ornaments is that which
they call a *Fuge*. This Ornament at this day is
moſt excellent, difficult, ingenuous, efficacious,
and full of Liberty. And this *Fuge* is nothing elſe
then a more artificial repetition and imitation of certain Parts: to which a more Simple Repetition and
Imitation is oppoſed, which alſo hath his Commen-
dations amongſt Muſicians. And this is the Example of a *Fuge* in the *Uniſon* after two *Times*.

Unum eſt neceſſarium.

* I ſuppoſe that this Example was miſtaken or rather miſ-placed by the Printer or ſome other, for I
cannot imagine that the Learned Authour would give
the Reader Four parts of Simple Counter-point,
for an Example of a *Fuge* in the *Uniſon* after two
Minims. Of which let this be an Example.

And thus the Compoſer may continue his *Fuge*
as long as he pleaſeth.

6. The *Exerciſe* of a *Fuge* is to begin in an Harmonical *Tryade* onely. For ſo other forms and *ſpecies* of
Fuges may more eaſily be apprehended. And for
Examples you may look amongſt thoſe Principal
and Heroick practical Muſicians, as *Orlandus* and
Marentius. Of which two, the one in his *Mot-
tets,* and the other in his *Madrigals,* hath brought *Me-
lopoeſie* to his higheſt pitch. There are latter Imita-
tors of theſe principal *Melopoets,* who notwithſtanding ought to have their due praiſe.

CHAP.

⊕⊕⊕⊕⊕⊕⊕⊕⊕⊕⊕⊕⊕⊕⊕⊕⊕⊕⊕⊕⊕⊕⊕⊕⊕

Chap. IX.

Of the Affections of an Harmo-nicall Song.

Precepts.

IN the laſt place the Affections of a muſicall Song do follow, wherewith it is affected and perfected.

And they are either material or foꝛmal.

The material Affection of a Song, is that which floweth from the matter thereof. And it is a certain Genus of Modulation.

The foꝛmal Affection of a Song, is that which floweth from the foꝛm there-of: and is called a muſical Trope oꝛ Mood; which is a Rule, accoꝛding to which we direct the courſe of a Song. Otherwiſe called Nomus and Tonus. And it is the ſame in Muſick, as a certain kind of verſe is in Poetry.

A

A muſical Mood is either ſimple or compounded.

The ſimple is primarie or ſecondarie. That is called Authentick, and this Plagal.

The primarie mood is either legitimate or ſpurious.

The legitimate is either more natural in a ſharp Scale, or more ſoft in a flat Scale. And both is threefold ; the Ionick, Lydian , Mixolydian , Dorian , Phrygian , and Æolian.

The ſpurious, baſtard, or illegitimate Mood is the Hyper-Æolian , and Hyper-Phrygian.

The ſecondary or Plagal Mood is alſo called remiſſe and ſubmiſſe: and it is Hypo-Ionic, Hypo-Doric, Hypo-Phrygian, HypoLydian,Hypo-Mixolydian,and Hypo-Æolic.

The compounded or connex Mood , is that which doth ariſe from ſimple Moods : when the Authent is joyned with the Plagal Mood : whence it is called the Plagio-ſyntactical-Trope.

RULES.

Rules.

1. *The mixed Genus of Modulation is now for the moſt part in uſe.*

The *Genus* of *Modulation* is certain, according unto which the Song doth proceed in his Melodies in a certain Muſical Scale. Therefore as the *Scale* of *Muſick* is ſimple, or mixed, and that old or new : (alſo the old *Scale* is either *Enharmonic,* or *chromatic,* or *diatonic :* the new, *Syntonic*) So alſo the *Genus* of Modulation is ſimple, or mix'd, or compounded : the ſimple is old or new : Again the old is *enharmonic, chromatic,* or *diatonic.* And is alſo called *Enharmoniſme, Chromatiſme,* and *Diatoniſme.* The new is *Syntonic* or *Syntoniſme.* The mixed *Genus* of Modulation is that which is variouſly compounded of the Simple. Of the Simple, at this Day, *Enharmoniſme* and *Chromatiſme* (to wit alone :) partly for their Imperfection, partly for their Difficulty are not in uſe ; but the *Syntonian-Diatoniſme,* or *Diaton-Syntoniſme,* yet ſo, that *chromatiſme* be often mixed, and ſometimes alſo *Enharmoniſme,* if there be need, according to the force and acuracy of the Text.

2. *A Muſical Mood is the moſt certain Rule of a Song.*

A muſical Mood is that, according to which a muſical Song is limited, and without it would be too ample and wandring. The Mood therefore doth contain Melody with certain Limits, and as it were Bounds of an ha. monical *Trias*, in the Compaſs of an *Octave* or *Diapaſon*; ſo that wholly it doth continually proceed in a due order, from the beginning, by the middle, to the end, for the artificial expreſ-ſing unto, and imprinting upon the hearers the vir-tue of the Text.

3. *The Doctrine of Moods is contained in theſe Rules.*

1. *We cannot moderate or modulate any Song, un-leſſe we firſt know the Tone thereof.* The *Tone* is known by the end, according to *Rule :* in the end it is ſeen of what *Tone* it is. The end alſo of a Song is judged by the muſical Mood, which therefore by ſome *is* called a *Tone*, according to this Diverſity of *Tones*, there are alſo divers *Melodies*. For as one *Tone* is in *vt*, and another in *re :* So alſo are the *Melodies*. Yet here you muſt remember, that every *Tone* or *Mood* may not only be known by the end, but alſo by the beginning, and middle or Diviſion thereof: alſo by his skipping. 2. *A muſical Mood*, *is an Octave*

Octave mediated by his neighbouring voice. Otherwiſe it is defined to be the Species of a *Diapaſon*, which is made up of a *Diateſſeron* and *Diapente*. 3. *The Simple Mood is that in which one harmonical Triade only doth rule with his Octave*, in reſpect of the *Text* and more ſimple *Affection*. 4. *All the Moods are ſix*, even as there are ſix voices. *vt. re. mi. fa. ſol. la.* The Ancients had only four *Moods*, the firſt, ſecond, third, and fourth : to which now the four final *Voices* do reſpond. *re. mi. fa. ſol.* Theſe four *Moods* the *Grecians* call *Authentic*, and the *Latines herile* or *Clamous*. For they have, as I may ſo ſpeak, a greater Authority of aſcending then the reſt. But the *Latines* more narrowly conſidering the aſcenſion and deſcenſion of every *Tone*, have conſtituted to every *Mood* a ſubjugal *Mood*; and thoſe four they call *Plagal*; alſo ſubjugal, ſervile, and the like. And theſe deſcend more then the firſt. And hence ariſe the eight Moods, by which every Song is governed *per Arſin & Theſin*, by riſing or falling. But our Latter *Muſicians* more diligently conſidering the variety of *Tones*, have conſtituted twelve legitimate *Tones. viz.* ſix Authent, and as many Plagal. For as there are ſix Voices. *vt. re. mi. fa. ſol. la.* ſo alſo there are ſix Authent, and as many Plagal, which are vulgarly named by ſtrange Names of Nations : I ſay, of thoſe Nations who commonly were delighted with them. And to theſe twelve legimate Tones, two illegitimate were added. Unto all which, various mixed Moods may be added. 5. *An Authent Mood is primary, the Plagal ſecondary*, and this doth not differ from that,

but

but in reſpect of ſubjection, when it is called *Hypo-*
tropus, remiſs and ſubmiſs, becauſe the harmonical
Mediation of the *Octave*, which doth agree with the
primary, is changed into the arithmetical, by the in-
verſion of the fourth beneath the fifth with the *Tri-*
ade. 6. *Concerning the Excellency and Efficacy of*
the muſical Moods, there are diverſe opinions. *Caſus*
in politicis lib. 8. chap. 5. ſaith thus, *Muſick is va-*
rious and manifold. One kind *is humble and remiſs,*
as the Lydian ; *another is vehement and more moved,*
as the Phrygian ; *another is more moderate and mean*
which is called the Doric ; and a little after, *that*
grave, divine, and oraculous Muſick, called the
Doric, *allureth the mind to the ſtudy of Wiſdome and*
true Piety. This, both the heathen of old uſed in
their Synagogues, and Chriſtians now uſe in their
Churches. For in it there is a certain imitation of
Celeſtial Harmony, by which as by a ſweet and whol-
ſome Medicine, the Diſeaſes of the mind are cu-
red, Vices are diſſipated, Cares are leſſened : and
the Dew of Divine *Grace* is leiſurely, and by little
and little diſtilled. And in the end of the Chapter,
he ſaith, *that the* Doric *Muſick hath reſpect unto*
Virtues, and divine Inſpiration; and that it forceth
men into Extaſie of mind, and oblivion of the world;
ſo that it driveth away evil Spirits, which he proveth
by the Example of Saul. Lippius in his muſical *Sy-*
nopſis, ſaith thus : *the moſt natural and chief of all*
the Moods in theſe times, is the Ionic, *with his ſecun-*
dary the HypoIonic. (againſt which many ancient
and modern Muſicians do ſpeak.) But let us look upon the nature of the Moods in Specie. 7. *The na-*
ture

ture of the Authent Moods is this. The *Authent Mood* hath his final Key in the *Diapente* below , and is divided harmonically. And that is called harmonical Diviſion , where the *Octave* hath the *Fifth* beneath the *Fourth* , thus ; Firſt the *Ionic* doth occur , which is by *Lucian* called *Glaphyrus. i. e.* pleaſant: and by *Apuleius* wanton. And now it is much uſed. It runneth between *C.* and *c.* is divided in *G.* and endeth in *c.* In a flat Song it runneth between *F.* and *f.* and is divided in *C.* and endeth in *f.* It is moſt agreeable to *Iambic's* and *Trochaic's.* Then the *Dorian* Mood runneth between *D.* and *d.* and is divided in *a.* ending in *d.* but raiſed , or in a flat Song, hath his courſe between *g.* and *gg.* and is divided in *d.* and endeth in *gg.* By *Lucian* it is called grave , and by *Apuleius* warlike. It is moſt fit to ſing to heroick Verſe : for it hath wonderful Gravity with Alacrity. The *Phrygian* Mood hath his courſe between *E.* and *e.* and is divided in *mi* which is in *b.* ending in *e.* In a flat Song it runneth between *a.* and *aa.* and is divided in *e.* and endeth in *a a.* *Lucian* calleth it *Entheus*, *Apuleius* religious. For it hath the ſevere Inſultation of an angry man, whence it is called *Scolius.* It is impetuous, accommodated to warlike Affairs. It is alſo *Iambic* and *tragic* ; diſtracting and raviſhing the mind, putting it as it were out of it ſelf , as *Ariſtotle* ſaith , 8. *pol. c.* 5. and *Plato* 3. *de Inſtit.* The *Lydian* Mood doth take his courſe between *F.* and *f.* is divided in *c.* and endeth in *f.* in a flat Song it runneth between *b.* and *bb.* and is divided in *f.* and endeth in *bb.* It is harſh, threatning , and merry. As *Plato* 3. *dial. de rep.* who

con·

condemneth the *Lydian* and *Ionic Harmony* as ſottiſh.
This Mood is ſharp, and according to *Apuleius*,
threatning: and to *Lucian Bacchicus.q.* raging. The
Mixolydian Mood runneth between *g.* and *gg.* and is
divided in *d.* and endeth in *gg.* In a flat Song it
runneth between *c.* and *cc.* and is divided in *gg.* And
endeth in *cc.* It moveth the Affections, and ren-
dreth them ſorrowful and contracted; becauſe it is
mingled with the *Dorick* gravity. Laſtly, the *Æ-
olian* Mood runneth between *a.* and *aa.* and is divided
in *e.* and endeth in *aa.* being raiſed up, it runneth
between *d.* and *dd.* and is divided in *aa.* and endeth
in *dd.* It is mild and very ſweet, being ſung to *Lyrick*
Verſes. 8. *The nature of the Plagal Moods is this.*
This Mood is called Plagal, as if we ſhould ſay ob-
lique or inverſed; which hath its final Key in the loweſt part of the fifth, but above the fourth: and is
divided arithmetically. That Diviſion is by *Muſicians* called arithmetical, Where the *Octave* hath
the fourth beneath the fifth; which is the more unpleaſant. This Mood borroweth his name from the
Authent, *Hypo* being prefixed thereunto. Firſt the *Hypoionic* Mood runneth between *r.* and *g.* and divideth
and endeth in *C.* being raiſed up, it runneth between
C. and *c.* it is divided in *F.* In this Mood, the Mo-
lity of the *Ionic* Mood is rectified. The *Hypodorian*
Mood runneth between *A.* and *a.* is divided and endeth in *D.* being raiſed up between *D.* and *d.* is
divided and endeth in *g.* It hath a harſh kind of
Gravity, and flattereth not. The *Hypophrigian*
Mood runneth between *B ſharp,* and *b ſharp,* is divided and ended in *E.* being raiſed up, it runneth between

tween *E.* and *e.* is divided and ended in *a.* This Mood
is humble, and inclineth to weeping, as making a
ſorrowful Complaining and pitiful Lamentation.
The *Hypolydian* Mood runneth between *C.* and *c.* is
divided and ended in *F.* being raiſed up it runneth between *F.* and *f.* is divided and ended in *b flat.* It
expreſſeth a kind of ſorrowful Continency, and is
called the pious, and as it were puling Mood; and
ſtirreth up tears. The *Hypomixolydian* Mood runneth between *D.* and *d.* is divided and ended in *g.*
being raiſed, it runneth between *G.* and *g.* is divided and ended in *c.* In it there is a certain natural
jollity. The *Hypo Æolian* Mood runneth between
E. and *e.* is divided and ended in *a.* being raiſed up,
it runneth between *a.* and *aa.* and is divided in *d.*
9. *This is the nature of the illegitimate Moods.* An
illegitimate or baſtard Mood, is that, which cannot aptly be divided into the fifth and fourth: but
into the *Tritone* and *Semidiapente.* And it is either
the *Hyper Æolian* Mood, or the *Hyperphrygian.*
The *Hyper Æolian* Mood is the illegitimate of the
Authent; which runneth between *b.* and *bb.* having
below a *Semidiapente*, and above a *Tritone.* The
Hyperphrygian is the Baſtard of the Plagal Mood,
which runneth between *F.* and *f.* having a *Tritone*
below, and a *Semidiapente* above. 10. *Every ſimple Mood, out of his own proper harmonical Triade,
doth give to every harmonical Song, peculiar Ornaments.* To wit, *Fuges* and *Cloſes* proper, primary, ſecundary, and tertiary. Unto which, ſtrange
Cloſes from a ſtrange *Triad* may be added; if they
be well taken. The primary *Fuge*, and alſo the
G *Cloſe*

Cloſe is from the firſt of his proper *Triade :* the Secondary from the higheſt : and the Tertiary from the
middle. 11. *Every Mood in reſpect of his Effect
and Affection , doth follow his Radix. i. e.* his *Monads, Dyads,* and *Trias* of which he doth confiſt.
Hence it is (ſaith Lippius) *that one Mood is very
cheerful and lively* ; as the *Ionic* very much , the *Lydian* devoutly ; the *Mixolydian* moderately ; another flat , ſoft, ſorrowful, and grave , as the *Doric*
meanly ; the *Æolian* leſſe ; and the *Phrygian* ex-
ceedingly. 12. *A compounded Mood doth proceed
from ſimple Moods , and from it a Song is called mixed.* A Mood is compounded of Moods neer unto
him , as the *Ionic* and *Hyper-Ionic* which is often
ſeen : or of Moods wholly diverſe, as the *Ionic* and
Doric ; which is leſſe uſed. This mixture dependeth more or leſſe upon the affected Text. 13. *The
Mood in inſtrumental Muſick , by the Mediation of Chromatiſme, is tranſpoſed either to the fourth
above ; or,* which is the ſame, *to the fifth beneath.*
Hence, from a regular or ſharp Mood , an irregular Mood is made , which is called *mollis.* It is
tranſpoſed alſo to the ſecond, third, or other Interval : So that one Mood is changed into the nature
of another ; as the *Lydian* , into the *Ionic :* the
Hypolydian into the *Hypo-Ionic.* 14. *Always the
two proximate Moods* (the Authent with his Plagal)
have the ſame fifth , and the ſame fourth. Thus,

I.

1 & 2.	*Quartam.*	re ſol.
	Quintam.	re la.
3 & 4.	*Quartam.*	mi la.
	Quintam.	mi mi.
5 & 6.	*Quartam.*	vt fa.
	Quintam.	fa fa.
7 & 8.	*Quartam.*	re ſol.
	Quintam.	vt ſol.
9 & 10.	*Quartam.*	re ſol.
	Quintam.	re la.
11 & 12.	*Quartam.*	vt fa.
	Quintam.	vt ſol.

But here let us place *Schemes* to illuſtrate this thing.

Authent Moods in a ſharp Song.

Authent Moods in a Flat Song.

Plagal Moods in a Sharp Song.

Of the *Plagal Mood in à Flat Song.*

By theſe Tables it doth appear that the Plagal Mood differeth not from the Authent but by remiſſion into the fourth : when in the Authent here is an Elevation into the fifth *v. g.* if in the *Ionic* Mood it be *vt, ſol,* in the *HypoIonic,* it will be *vt. fa.* hence alſo the Compaſs of all Moods may eaſily be found.

v. gr.

v. gr. the Compaſs of the *Ionic* Mood in a *ſharp* Song, is *ſol. vt.* in a flat Song *fa. vt.* the Compaſs of the *Dorian* Mood in a *ſharp* Song is *re. la.* in a flat Song *re. ſol.* and ſo of the reſt.

⊕⊕⊕⊕⊕⊕⊕⊕⊕⊕⊕⊕⊕⊕⊕⊕⊕⊕⊕⊕⊕⊕⊕⊕⊕⊕⊕

Chap. X.

Of Special Muſick.

Precepts.

THus far of the general part of Muſick : the ſpecial remaineth, concerning the various kinds of Muſick, which are taken either from the matter : oʒ the Character of the matter : oʒ the Organical Cauſe : oʒ Artifice of Muſick.

First, From the Matter, Muſick is either ſacred oʒ civil.

Secondly, From the Character, Muſick is either great, oʒ mean, oʒ humble.

Thirdly, From the Organical Cauſe, Muſick is vocal, inſtrumental, oʒ mixed. That is made by the voice of man, the next by divers Inſtruments, and this

by

by the Voice and Instrument together.

Fourthly, from Artifice, Muſick is either Choral or Figural. That doth in his Notes obſerve an equal meaſure, and from the Author is called Gregorian : and this is either old or plaine.

This is ſuch whoſe unequal Notes do vary their meaſure, and from the Author is called Ambroſian.

Alſo menſural, and new Muſick.

Rules.

1. *The aſper Artery [or Windpipe] of a man, Vocal by the Tongue, is the Law of all Muſical Inſtruments.*

Lively or Vocal Muſick as they call it, ſeeing it is the Cauſe of Inſtrumental Muſick, without Controverſie is the nobleſt of all. And if it be joyned with inſtrumental Muſick, it is an incredible Means of moving the Affections and Sences. Alſo Vocal Muſick is called the Exemplary or paradigmatical Cauſe of Inſtrumental Muſick : whatſoever they talk of *Pythagoras*, that he found out Muſick by the ſtriking of divers Hammers upon an *Anvile*.

2. *A Song which may be ſung both by Voice and Inſtrument , is various.*

To this belongeth a *Mottet* , *Madrigal*, *Imtrade*, and bound *Fuge :* and this of one harmonical *Triade* only, or of more. Alſo the *uniſonous Simply* , or *multiſonous* . and that through the *eight* , *fifth* , *third*, &c. Alſo to theſe may be referred Songs of one , two , three, four, or five Voices, and like-wiſe Songs of many Voices, or *Polyphoniacs :* which for their perfection may ſwell to forty or more Melodies. Of theſe the Song for one Voice is an harmonical Song potentially : the Song for two Voices, is the firſt harmonical Song , in Act ; but more imperfect : but the Song for three Voices is perfecter : and the Song of four voices moſt perfect.

3. *Muſical Inſtruments may conveniently be reduced to theſe two kinds.*

For ſome are called *Pſhelaphetus :* and others are called *Pneumatic :* and theſe are called *Croſta's* , which only by ſtriking do make a Concent, and by others are called *Entata.* Theſe are alſo called *Empneuſta* , and they are moved with the Fingers and Wind. Various kinds of Inſtruments are comprehended under theſe. As the *Whiſtle*, *Pipe*, *Cornet*, *Sackbut*, *Trumpet* , *Bagpipe* , and the like, which are blown. Alſo the *Clavichord* , *Pſaltery* , *Pandore ,*

dore, *Cithren*, and the like, which are ſtruck with ſtrings: So alſo the *Lute*, *Harp*, *Lyre*, *Tabor*, and other Inſtruments ſtruck with ſtrings. The *Cymbal*, *great Bell*, and others ſtruck with Braſs. Alſo the muſical *Triangle* ſtruck with Iron or Steel. Or the Wooden *Craticle* (by the *Germans* called *einſtroſiedel' item ein holtzerngelachter*) ſtruck with Wood. And laſtly the great Wind Inſtrument or *Organ* which is both blown and ſtruck together. And here it will be neceſſary to lay down certain *Aphoriſmes* concerning muſical Inſtruments. 1. *The Canon*, *Mother*, *and Radix of all Inſtruments*, *is the Monochord:* which is an Inſtrument moſt ſimple, and intire, made of one or more *uniſonous Chords*; and may be divided into how many, or how great parts you pleaſe, according to radical numbers by the *bipartition*, *tripartition*, *quadripartition*, &c. thereof. And we may obſerve fully in this Inſtrument, all the proportions of all muſical numbers. And this will be the moſt ſimple Example of a *Monochord*, if you ſhall put one Chord upon a fit peice of Wood; into ſo many parts as you ſhall divide the Wood, certain Notes being added, ſo many diſtinct Sounds there will be, if you apply your finger to the Chord. 2. *The Wooden Craticle is next in plaineſſe unto the Monochord.* This is made reaſy without any trouble, if a Wooden ſtick being very drie, be proportionably divided into many parts; which according to the Order of Proportions, being bound together by links made of a ſtring, do afford harmonical Sounds, if they be ſtruck with a ſtick, and put to ſtraw bound together. 3. *The Lute is the chiefeſt of all Inſtru-*

ments of Muſick. For no Invention of ancient or modern Muſicians did ever make a more gratefulconcent. 4. *In Clavichords and the like Inſtruments there is the moſt evident Reaſon of the Scale of Muſick.* Thoſe Inſtruments do conſiſt of certain *Tetrachords,* which are double, ordinary, and extraordinary. The ordinary *Tetrachords* are four. The firſt is called *Hypaton i. e.* of greater and graveſt Chords : from *B.* to *E.* and this is the *Baſs.* The *Second* is *Meſon,* *i. e.* of *Means:* from *E.* to *a.* and this is the *Tenor.* It is called *Meſon,* becauſe in old time when there were only three *Tetrachords,* (the *Tetrachord Hyperbolæon* not being added) it was in the midſt. The third is *Diezeugmenon* of diſtinct *Chords,* which is disjoyned from *a.* by a *Tone,* which is from *b.* to *e.* and this is the *Altus.* The fourth is *Hyperbolæon i. e.* of excellent or moſt acute *Chords :* from *e.* to *aa.* and this is the *Diſcantus.* The extraordinary *Tetrachord* is *Synemmenon. i. e.* of connexed Chords; ſo called becauſe it is joyned with *a.* and it extendeth from *a.* to *d.* There is alſo a threefold progreſſion of theſe *Tetrachords,* viz. *diatonic,* *enharmonic,* and *chromatic.* The *diatonic* progreſſion is by a *Ditonus* and leſſer *Semitone.* The *enharmonic* by a *Ditonus* and two *Dieſes, viz,* the greater and leſſer *Dieſis. i. e.* the half of the leſſer *Semitone.* And the *chromatic* progreſſion is made by the *Semiditone,* and greater and leſſer *Semitones.* (*vide triple Scale chap.* 5.) This Doctrine will be clearer, if the Doctrine of Sounds, or muſical Intervalls, or Moods (as they vulgarly call them) be rightly propounded. For there are in all Ten Moods according to a known

Song. *The Moods are three times three , and one , by which every Song is made.* ſc. *The Uniſon , Semitone, Tone, Semiditone, Ditone, Diateſſaron , Diapente, Semitone with a Diapente , Tone with a Diapente , Diapaſon.* And whoſoever ſhall diligently conſider theſe Moods , ſhall eaſily know the *Ration* of muſical *Intervalls* , and ſo of all *Harmony.* And the Artificial Diviſion of theſe Moods is this. A *Mood,* or rather a Sound , is an Intervall or Diſtance from another, and that is either equal or unlike. An equal *Mood* is that which is in the ſame Degree, and is called the *uniſon* or *Baſis.* Alſo an *Uniſon* is the conjunction of two or more Notes in the ſame place. *e. gr.* if *ſol* be repeated in the ſame Key , or *la,* the *Mood* is unlike, in which there is both *Arſis* and *Theſis. i. e.* Elevation and Demiſſion of the Sound. And this is either continued or interrupted. A continued Sound is a *Tone* or *Semitone.* A *Tone* is the skipping of a Voice from a Voice by a perfect Second ſounding ſtrongly.   Hence it is called a Second.   In the progreſſion of ſix muſical Voices, every next is diſtant from his next by a *Tone. e. gr. vt re.* except *mi fa* joyned together ; which Connexion is called a *Semitone,* which is the skipping of the Voice into a Voice by an imperfect Second, ſounding flatly : as is the Leaping from *mi* into *fa* , and again from *fa* into *mi. ſcil.* the next. By the *Greeks* it is called *Hemitone :* and by *Muſicians* the leſſer *Semitone.* The interrupted Mood is diſcrete by certain Intervalls. The firſt is *Diaphonus,* as the *Ditonus* and *Semiditonus.* The *Ditonus* is a ſharp and perfect third : and doth conſiſt of two *Tones* , as is between *vt mi. fa la.* otherwiſe therwife called the *Third*. The *Semiditonus* is the Intervall of the Voice from a Voice by a flat and imperfect Third. As between *re fa. mi fol*. The Second is *Paraphonus*. As a *Diateffaron* and a *Diapente*. A *Diateffaron* is the leaping from a Voice into a Voice by a fourth. As is between *vt fa. re fol.* and *mi la*. otherwife called a fourth. The *Diapente* is the skipping of a Voice from a Voice by a Fifth : called vulgarly *Quadrimode* and *Quinta*. As between *vt fol. re la. mi mi. fa fa*. And again a Fifth is either compounded with a *Tone* or a *Semitone*. Hence a *Tone* with a *Diapente* is a perfect Sixth, as is between *vt* from *c* to *la* in *a*. The *Semitone* with a *Diapente* is the imperfect *Sixth*. As between *mi* from *e* to *fa* in *c*. and contrarily. The Third is *Antiphonus*. as the *Diapafon :* which is the Diftance of a Voice from a Voice by an Eighth ; whence it is called an *Octave*. And it is made feven wayes *i. e.* from every Letter to his like ; as from *A* to *a*. from *a* to *aa*. &c. To thefe *Moods* or *Intervalls* there are four prohibited *Intervalls* oppofed by vulgar Muficians. 1. A *Tritone* which containeth three *Tones*, and is made from *fa* to *mi*. 2. A *Semidiapente* which paffeth from *mi* to *fa*. containing two *Tones* and as many *Semitones*. 3. A *Semidiapafon*, which is an *Octave* containing three *Semitones* and four *Tones*, reaching from *mi* to *fa*. 4. A *Difdiapafon*, which is an *Intervall* by a Fifteenth ; within which there is a Limit appointed to the Voice: beyond which it may not wander ; and if it wander it is but feigned ; For if more Diftances then a *Diapafon* occur, they will equifonate with the former *Diftances* in the *Octave*.

Conclufion.

Concluſion.

AND this is the *MUSICAL TEMPLE*, whoſe Foundation is *Harmony*, or *Concord*: whoſe Covering is honeſt *Pleaſure*: whoſe Wood and Stones are the Harmonical *Monads*, *Dyads*, and *Tryads*. That thou mayeſt not only enter this *Temple*, but build thy ſelf; after the diligent reading of this *Synopſis* which we here preſent thee with: Conſider thoſe *melopoetic Claſſic's* and prime Muſicians, *Orlandus* and *Marentius*. But chiefly exercise thy ſelf in the *Analyſis* of many examples; and then from that betake thy ſelf to the muſical *Synthesis*.

FINIS.